O Cidadán

ALSO BY ERIN MOURÉ/EIRIN MOURE

Sheep's Vigil by a Fervent Person: A Translation of Alberto Caeiro/
Fernando Pessoa's O Guardador de Rebanhos
Pillage Laud
A Frame of the Book, a.k.a. *The Frame of a Book*
Search Procedures
The Green Word: Selected Poems 1973-1992
Sheepish Beauty, Civilian Love
WSW (West South West)
Furious
Domestic Fuel
Wanted Alive
Empire, York Street

O Cidadán

poems

Erín Moure

Anansi

Published in 2002 in Canada
and in the United States in 2003 by
House of Anansi Press Limited
895 Don Mills Rd., 400-2 Park Centre
Toronto, ON, M3C 1W3
Tel. 416-445-3333
Fax 416-445-5967
www.anansi.ca

Distributed in Canada by
General Distribution Services Ltd.
325 Humber College Blvd.
Etobicoke, ON, M9W 7C3
Tel. 416-213-1919
Fax 416-213-1917
E-mail cservice@genpub.com

05 04 03 02 01   1 2 3 4 5

National Library of Canada Cataloguing in Publication Data

Mouré, Erin, 1955–
O Cidadan

Poems.
ISBN 0-88784-674-2

I. Title.

PS8576.O96O3 2002   C811'.54   C2002-900332-6
PR9199.3.M68O3 2002

Text Design: Tannice Goddard
Cover Image: Lani Maestro

THE CANADA COUNCIL | LE CONSEIL DES ARTS
FOR THE ARTS | DU CANADA
SINCE 1957 | DEPUIS 1957

*We acknowledge for their financial support of our
publishing program the Canada Council of the Arts, the Ontario
Arts Council, and the Government of Canada through the
Book Publishing Industry Development Program (BPIDP).*

Printed and bound in Canada

To intersect a word: citizen. To find out what could intend/distend it, today. *O cidadán.* A word we recognize though we know not its language. It can't be found in French, Spanish, Portuguese dictionaries. It seems inflected "masculine." And, as such, it has a feminine supplement. Yet if I said "a cidadá" I would only be speaking of 52% of the world, and it's the remainder that inflects the generic, the *cidadán.* How can a woman then inhabit the general (visibly and semantically skewing it)? How can she speak from the generic at all, without vanishing behind its screen of transcendent value? In this book, I decided, I will step into it just by a move in discourse. I, a woman: o cidadán. As if "citizen" in our time can only be dislodged when spoken from a "minor" tongue, one historically persistent despite external and internal pressures, and by a woman who bears – as lesbian in a civic frame – a *policed sexuality.* Unha cidadán: a semantic pandemonium. If a name's force or power is "a *historicity* . . . a sedimentation, a repetition that congeals," (Butler) can the name be reinvested or infested, fenestrated . . . set in motion again? Unmoored? Her semblance? Upsetting the structure/stricture even momentarily. *To en(in)dure, perdure.*

To move the force in any language, create a slippage, even for a moment . . . to decentre the "thing," unmask the relation . . .

Facturusne operae pretium sim si a primordio urbis res populi Romani perscripserim nec satis scio nec, si sciam, dicere ausim, quippe qui cum veterem tum volgatam esse rem videam, dum novi semper scriptores aut in rebus certius aliquid allaturos se aut scribendi arte rudem vetustatem superaturos credunt. Utcumque erit, iuvabit tamen rerum gestarum memoriae principis terrarum populi pro virili parte et ipsum consuluisse; et si in tanta scriptorum turba mea fama in obscuro sit, nobilitate ac magnitudine eorum me qui nomini officient meo consoler. Res est praeterea et immensi operis, ut quae supra septingentesimum annum repetatur et quae ab exiguis profecta initiis eo creverit ut iam magnitudine laboret sua; et legentium plerisque haud dubito quin primae origines proximaque originibus minus praebitura voluptatis sint, festinantibus ad haec nova quibus iam pridem praevalentis populi vires se ipsae conficiunt: ego contra hoc quoque laboris praemium petam, ut me a conspectu malorum quae nostra tot per annos vidit aetas, tantisper certe dum prisca illa tota mente repeto, auertam, omnis expers curae quae scribentis animum, etsi non flectere a uero, sollicitum tamen efficere posset.

Quae ante conditam condendamve urbem poeticis magis decora fabulis quam incorruptis rerum gestarum monumentis traduntur, ea nec adfirmare nec refellere in animo est. Datur haec venia antiquitati ut miscendo humana divinis primordia urbium augustiora faciat; et si cui populo licere oportet consecrare origines suas et ad deos referre auctores, ea belli gloria est populo Romano ut cum suum conditorisque sui parentem Martem potissimum ferat, tam et hoc gentes humanae patiantur aequo animo quam imperium patiuntur. Sed haec et his similia utcumque animaduersa aut existimata erunt haud in magno equidem ponam discrimine: ad illa mihi pro se quisque acriter intendat animum, quae vita, qui mores fuerint, per quos uiros quibusque artibus domi militiaeque et partum et auctum imperium sit; labente deinde paulatim disciplina velut desidentes primo mores sequatur animo, deinde ut magis magisque lapsi sint, tum ire coeperint praecipites, donec ad haec tempora quibus nec uitia nostra nec remedia pati possumus perventum est. Hoc illud est praecipue in cognitione rerum salubre ac frugiferum, omnis te exempli documenta in inlustri posita monumento intueri; inde tibi tuaeque rei publicae quod imitere capias, inde foedum inceptu foedum exitu quod vites. Ceterum aut me amor negotii suscepti fallit, aut nulla unquam res publica nec maior nec sanctior nec bonis exemplis ditior fuit, nec in quam ciuitatem tam serae avaritia luxuriaque immigraverint, nec ubi tantus ac tam diu paupertati ac parsimoniae honos fuerit. Adeo quanto rerum minus, tanto minus cupiditatis erat: nuper diuitiae auaritiam et abundantes voluptates desiderium per luxum atque libidinem pereundi perdendique omnia invexere. Sed querellae, ne tum quidem gratae futurae cum forsitan necessariae erunt, ab initio certe tantae ordiendae rei absint: cum bonis potius ominibus votisque et precationibus deorum dearumque, si, ut poetis, nobis quoque mos esset, libentius inciperemus, ut orsis tantum operis successus prosperos darent.

Contents

montréal papers

roof papers, Rachel-Julien

parc Jeanne-Mance papers

a chapter on reading

"fugitivo"

no paraíso do sono

na cidade papers

fleuve portal

10 do novembro de 2001
Montréal, au Rachel-Julien, *sans emma*
Erín Moure

In homage to the poetic work, which is civic work, in my country, of
Phyllis Webb
Robin Blaser

and to the work of
44904, le stukkateur, Jorge Semprún
Agnès Varda
and to two young Africans who tried to call out to Europe,
with the body (mortos) of writing (escritas nos seus petos):
Yaguine Koita and Fodé Tounkara

« . . . en las condiciones actuales de transformación de los conceptos básicos de comprensión del Estado nacional – territorio, soberanía, explicación completa de la sociedad desde sí y para sí misma – no existen interioridades puras ni exterioridades completas. Y en su lugar debemos aprender a pensar con conceptos como los de complejidad, implicación en diversidad de ámbitos, pluralismo institucional, multi-referencialidad de las identidades y de las identificaciones. »

Joseba Arregi
quoted in *El País*, 30 September 1998

"An ailing nationalism can only recover through the force of abstraction."
Fernando Vallespín, *El País*, 15 January 2001

"When pushed to the wall, art is too slow."
Lisa Robertson, "Thursday," *The Weather*

Georgette

Georgette thou burstest my deafness
woe to the prosperities of the world

because I am not yet full of thee I am but a burthen
to myself

Thou breathedst odours, and I drew in breath and
did pant for thee, I tasted and did hunger, where thou
hast touchedst me I did burn
for peace

time's subject motional and "form"
a code of vinyl
bar's emphasis

there yet live in my memory the images of such things

the hearse upon a station
a cross upon a fear
an insigne upon a hearth

folio
::::::::::
adore

My Volition's Faint Trill

to my tops

A citizen uncorks uncertainty's mien.

Both (beckon) hesitate: will frequency stain her pattern
our key widely prepares?

+++

In the video memory, a witness on flesh between the cure is
every guest.
As the citizen was her, she raced a ripe space in the letter.

The seizure of speech tonics the her traits.

What about the trait produced by machine,
is it without intention?

The idiom blew shut. *A brasa.*

Cloth is the thing. Dresses have drifted, and speech unbuttons my thing.

A brasa.

Why wouldn't saw sing? Seeing her? To swerve continues my slip,
and mountains – my decades – are experiments in beloved detail.

+++

To connect is so unconquerable a citizen only a gift may vibrate.

Prospect was their disease.

Every marked page was style.

Our essay changed.

The swish. Catalpa coalesce. ~~Sweet catalpa, moi cariña.~~
_____~~Sweet catalpa, Federico.~~
_____~~Sweet catalpa, Federico.~~
_____~~Sweet catalpa, Federico.~~
_____~~Sweet catalpa, Federico.~~
_____~~Sweet catalpa, Federico.~~
_____~~Sweet catalpa, Federico.~~
_____~~Sweet catalpa, Federico.~~
_____~~Sweet catalpa, Federico.~~
_____~~Sweet catalpa, Federico.~~

What do my shapes break? So past
a reaction through the atom of wit grieves.

+++

Duty: a process. A piece of stuff. A volition.
Shades around the citizen: its dresses.

+++

The birth of laughter was the essay.

Catalogue of the Harms

29 September 1998, Huddersfield, W. Yorkshire

Harmonic splendour, she thought.
Her armistice day that line across a field or path.
To mean is to weigh   *before that fret enactment*

such harm, to weigh the least of

Harm's imagery. "It was there I remembered" a
clue (to be turned from . . .)

To whom harm was done it may concern

> Debt's harm
> Depth'

Debit (a ditch where they buried the shot children) who is human

Her torn muscle in the arm
's shoulder that makes "shaking hands" difficult
An extensibility of the body into a world

It starts soon

It wings up and down it wears roses on its crown it play a merry maid it rest
breathless where it laid, it takes Paris's feint tower

At that moment, she remembered "Sharon Thesen"
Hermetic lines of such fraught discursibility

to imagine why this is: her resistible wound
is harm's rubric
a fleuve no why can entertain
harsh entry make, into a private integument

"to rend"
"harmless"

document1

Is the Cidadán a prosthetic gesture (across "languages")?

The capacity to "be affected by" is one of the things that make up the citizen. The C a bundle of affect, affectability (Spinoza, that *fillo marrán* of forced emigrations). Her harsh dead limb of language. Is the Cidadán a prosthetic gesture, across languages? Yet sensibility, affect, is always local. (J-L Nancy) Without locality there is no sensibility.

But what if the local, the notion of the local, is forever altered. Am I local *here* in my unease. "My Yorkshire" is a pediment of unease. These ties of adoration elsewhere, ties of affect. Can we even say "ties of affect."

The citizen is a mobile complex of: (Nancy again) rights, obligations, dignities, and virtues.

The citizen is just an enactment across prosthetic boundaries?
Or within them?

You be the judge. Pandemonium.

(what pandemonium entails)

prosthesis pandemonium gesture suture

Georgette

For you, Georgette, my reddened flower
base or if to glow
her wanton reach or smile (we saw)
she turned one leg it was a feeling "doll"

At the long path before the loss of graves
into a yellow corn

my heart you see its yellow corn
Girl I am, interpret

Or the one I walked with when I first saw your soft engrave
Hot Paris day of an arrival into Montparnasse with K

"waking into the her salt"

document2 (inaugural)

As if we are that dichogamous flower, each of us. Nancy locates the
resistances of sense as a "touching on the confines of the world." How to
write the sense of the world? Our cared selves a product always of
migrations or emigrative qualities, out of, a surge within a name burst open
like a pod of light in which we see Vigo or Londres, the small path along
the wall behind which are rows of vines. An *existentiale* of worldliness,
says Nancy: resistance to the closure of worlds within the world.

O cidadán a seal or bond with this world, nothing to do with country or
origin. The cidadán stands in time as the person stands in space, liquid
edge before or beyond the other she craves, the she she craves also a she,
and this is space that opens time,
> it is a space
> where time tumbles backwards, *brings a* future *into* presence

A public space is where we are both signs, O Claire. Our epochal
inclination.

> (Where "the court of agriculture is the border of grace,"
"shouting eliminates governors.")

proclitic enclitic diaeresis dias technē

Georgette

Dignified is a heartsong here
Harsh traverse of the unknown

"Better to go down dignified"
Ekes out
constant

What gives in us, or won't give
(her smile seen once in the Red Café)

Turns sparkless
Into sparklers

One "s" less
One "r" more, Georgette

-- -- -- -- --

The new wall we built that year
where the house side had been torn out

Grammar we called in

like a bet on narrative

-- -- -- -- --

Now I am the only one who hasn't yet gone in;
and I have these sentences

(fissures in the hand)

Second Catalogue of the Substitution of Harms*

		√		

harm	harm	harm	harm	harm
-------	-------	√	-------	-------
forms	term	devices	units	count

harm	harm	harm	harm	harm
-------	-------	-------	-------	√
world	bath	abs	kid	advised

harm	harm	harm	harm	harm
-------	-------	-------	-------	-------
arm	mayors	pain	nother	comedies

harm
----
influenced

*in the form of ~~functions~~ fractions

document3 (hieratic and paternal)

To resist the "hieratic and paternal" pose of touch – of access to a surface as
appropriation (à la Heidegger); think touch, rather, as quiver or thresholding,
mark and threshold//

For "without this (N) implacable reticulation of contiguities and tangential
contacts . . .

(EXALTATION POUR L : LYING STILL)

Amato is a harsh spatialization doubt conducts her ligature
Amato conducts doubt's fortuity her ligat
Element's ducts forewhet her lyre rake

Toy rake to wing

Fastidy nor trail of   fond fortuity
Her hope of breath to breathe   conducts her ligature
To digress

. . . there would be no world"

energeia entelecheia transport parousia gram

Georgette

Remembering the day the house was filled with snow
and business samples

Her couraget amenable to a sp;ur

Or to solidify:

"a penny for the guy" is just begging
come back when you have a proper guy

*

To solidify lyric flow
Those portable madnesses   syllables   I loved them
(how I loved them)

Soft and sudden lyric flow
describe

my writers' fond of each   surround *so shy*

as in L's: "I felt exalted"
which is to say
the exhaustion of alerted symptoms

*

Also wed to me is "harm's" bestowal
for an ecstatic gesture is perhaps not harm
harm's light in blood is veneration

Georgette   my fond alloy

her open fluid to my hand or eye
a visibility hence unendured but "féerique"
esa   lão   matá   al   oy

Third Catalogue of the Temperament of Harms

café	yellow	over	cliff	mandible
-------	-------	-------	-------	-------
forms	royd	devices	wit	vitables

heart	Cromwell	√	Corpus	Christi
-------	-------	-------	-------	-------
world	bade	abs	roe	devised

ex	wye	insurge	root	hospitable
-------	-------	-------	-------	-------
arm	mayors	by	nother	torrent

witters
----
influenced

```
café                            cliff mandible
yellow            over          Corpus Christi
heart Cromwell                  ex wye



              insurge          root    witters
*                               *
```

W. Yorkshire, October 1998
she were there for nought
were

vigour
endure

her entelecheia

(a drawing of a face)

document4 (weights)

"The units of weight" and their "frank" exchange. To say "the resistance to
the unacceptable [unha cidadán, for example] itself ought to proceed from
another sense," invokes submission/domination as a frank meeting of two
potentates, in a cut edge of undecidability, for submission's band turns (a
möbius)

and compels,
invites to, insists on being met, calls forth "want" urgency in the other and
fond display or concoctability of this urgency as "form"

"amid"

To construct the self is to be amid (necessitate) (prior?) civic space
or coil

Horticulture in a pear   her constraint is "pearls" to preen
hollow way
A further price to whey anatomy whose curl of light

There was an extension after what we heard
Guess a prologue   an immense chorale

(who signed this)

(are awakened)

invertebrate inveterate fallacy accuse

Fourth Catalogue of the Underwater Locker of Thieved Harms

Did harms' encyclical hold us in?
We compelled such harms, they said, like *bruxas*.

Mark's surface marked; mark
being where script endures

Fearless ambiguities in the clause.
A "wet" "fromage"

What I wrote in you, written against
all harm, and you the wettening surface
I declare upon
not advisedly but with splendours

and drapery; Velázquez risen from a Spanish tomb
to represent your dress

against the wet "fond" risen of that drapery
I raise above your knee

when I ask of you to lease caress
squatting upon my hand's murmur

or insistenence a trail
to become

unheld by that confine or boundary

(Egress me here)

(or ease)

(this frank equivalence

Georgette

What starts as a doubt
within the membrane of a fissure
within the unspeakable apparatus
of the membrane
can become a woman
Yesterday

years before us

A wit's world for example
a level used to measure
the accuracy of a wall's construct
our corporeal wall or construct
device used for imperative projection
before the cornucopic ectopy
the simultaneous legacy or legislative
quality

Years later   a body   does this

illustrate
To illustrate

document5 (dehiscence' tiny cape)

Cixous reads Clarice Lispector's *Paixão* as *aproximação* – approach or approximation – and it is political: the "between-us" which we must touch with care. Here, too, Nancy: "The word *world* has no unity of sense other than this one: a world is always a differential articulation of singularities that make sense in articulating themselves,

along the edges of their articulation . . ."

What if we all craved a poetic document, exquisitely worked each word a lattice of ingenuity? I don't believe this. To make sense is perhaps, as I read, to be susceptible to indication (not *definition*). If I were the tiny cape, you were your entries below another highway in the year of oxidation. What is allowable beyond a certain measure. Contiguous without absorption. As if to show you what I am wearing:

a	b	c	d	e	f	g	h	i	j	k l
m	n	o	p	q	r	s	t	u	v	w
x	y	z								

------- ------- ------- -------

her article to touch or not her article.

my lips miss "kindred"

Zinc bar on the rue de Rennes (Au Vieux Colombier)

Salt. Amorousness. A cliff or cleft, or wind.

Boundary or knee. rain

<98.11.12/Paris>

document6 (originary)

Is there an originary marking? If there were, would we be able to "read" it at all? Or does such a "trait" receive its function as mark only <u>from our reading</u>, our imposition of acculturated being that takes place in reading's gesture. And is thereby not "originary."

Even a fold in paper (as in a Micah Lexier marking˙) already cups will or deliberation. But how small such deliberations may be! ML's fold or cut at 36/75 of a simple page, it is both lexicon and auto-bio-graph-eme.

But "originary marking" – what would that be? A leaf's mark in stone? A twig fallen onto a stone, eroded differently because of this touch or -eme? But if I *see* the mark or fold in stone, that small cup in the river's sandstone (for it was once a lake) "like an ear," already my reading is what creates it as "trait," no?

Therefore, "not originary."

˙reference to one of ML's 1997 portraits on 8.5 x 11 paper: "Self-portrait as a piece of paper divided proportionately between the top area representing life lived and the bottom area representing life to come, based on statistical life expectancy. This piece of paper has been demarcated in the following manner: scored and folded completely over" document7 (outside)

Even *if* reading creates the trait, aren't *both* gestures needed? Isn't the *gestural* crossing of "reading" with "trait" the very armature of the trait as marking? The origin of any particular condensation of meaning is thus outside the body of the fold or mark, and outside the body of the reader, at a gestural point or series (temporal) of points that are traversed and that traverse (both active and passive). A kind of movement, then, *lisp-ecto-real.*

Which beckons the whole notion of "outside" into the field of inquiry and unseats it. For if the condensation that marks a trait as trait falls *outside* of the body or bodies of both, what is "inside"? What is "in" that must be kept "in" so badly that "outside" must be denominated as function? For here it bears functional value, not just prepositional (for the preposition is "repeated"). What is being split from what here?

Shall their narrative silicone prepare them for the bed of meats?

Torquēre pandemonium virtue coalesce

Georgette

for L, 8 January 1999

To think a "leaf" Georgette
Expect anatomy to interject

What does it *do* to "do"?
The "I exist" played out in draft or coin

100% elect array
A shadow on a grey-scale road between that moor

Up's density hill
Your torque my gleam from here avail

To wit: anatomy of "her" configuration
Cone drift amaze

To put the clamp myself on such my
labial tendency

awash
adore

the chain's connect or weight
to hold or open

"outside"
that anatomy "to be" (erinnerung)

Fifth Topology of the Renaissance of Harms

"chaque homme porte la forme entière de la humaine condition"

Michel de Montaigne, *Essais*, III ii

"je le prends à l'envers"   Engiatnom ed Lehcim

aultres	vrayement	sçay	tousjours	tantost
-------	-------	√	-------	-------
disoit	joyeulx	estoit	compaignon	mesme

quoy	regardans	animant	cecy	sçavante
-------	-------	-------	-------	√
moy	poinct	estre	bastir	besoing

fay	aage	chascun	espaule	nostre
-------	-------	-------	-------	-------
celuy	or	estoit	escoute	faict

conduictes

----

sçauray

"without syntactic vinculae"

document8 (constitutive fiction)

Lyotard speaks of trait or mark as "friction on the retina" "constitutive of seeing." To search a *first* or originary mark, then, could such yearning invite fascism? For always a mark precedes the mark; *this mark* here has a trait that precedes it. Visage touched by the hand. Frictive. That hand also linked, through arm, chest and neck, to a face. In turn, these features are imprinted on another hand. *Aproximação.* Here, no transcendence and no first mark; none is needed. And it will not insist on immanence either (-i- being the force of humanism, a last vigour wrenched from it by Heidegger). The wound throat possibly appeared, where the screen of affection was sleeping.

Visage   irremediable is my desire to
in the hand   embrace
borne wherein   not thwarted

outward   but to embrace the irremedial,
facing the planet (it is to face)   a sill's

an idiom snow   heart - fracas felt
-------   -------
to whet conjure   in the instance of a doorway

                                                stands within
                                                standing

soportar

Georgette

tardily entrance me now
her sill

her hand bearing shock of what my
mandible

a jaw or seer
copious

hand's mandible to the
why

+

Sixth Catalogue of the Pubis of Harms

there were places where we were cast aside
our grip was cast aside

irregular

justice to commit (to) memory – here conflate
memory's ripe mandible (face or pubis' prise)

> fo(u)nd
> in parents

---

feeling mild
's way to convey

host   guest
though
sometimes host is involuntary, tied

---

false idiom
----
to conjure

or satisfy « demeure »

to connive or to confer
"villagers"
"ás aldeas"
"arredores"

what are roots but wanderers in search of food
searching less bitter soil

Did so western a tale influence
the missile of peace?

light itself is monumental That
her visitor "interferes" with the work,   is the work

hers toff or   "residue"   is the work
Here words are used to "induce viewing"

"used to" can be read as custom here
distaff emblem
capability's demeanour   as aspect

---

starts here
                         rapture
                         rupture
                         rature

wine in cups

document9 (categorical resistance)

How is a trait "constitutive of seeing"? Lyotard insists that "reading the line in the letter evokes an unrecognizable activity, a seeing devoid of any meaning, underlying the claim to decipher the letter as recognizable meaning . . ." And further: "the very literalness of the letter functions as a figural or rhetorical excess over 'literal' meaning, an excess that is, moreover, constitutive of its very meaning." (Bill Readings)

As if, then, to exhibit harms is not to *describe* but to present exactly that rhetorical bind [excess] at which reading breaks. Thus: *fractions* as a visible/visual presentation, the line of the letter on an axis that is a will or intentionality.

"Therefore there is no way to conceptualize the encounter: it is made possible by the other, the unforeseeable 'resistant to all categories.'" (D)

How to think along the edges of something that is not yet a thing, using one's own "not yet" which is anterior to our "our"ness, to any "my" or any *sum* . . . and which creates the "our"ness too as a further (always further) "not-yet" superimposed or perhaps coalescent with an "our" that is tentative (but oh this is beauty) and urged up and forward by the "not-yet"

A grown admit will self or wander
(contra Heidegger)

The abruptness of necessity's coil
Harsh fact of it

Homily she asked was not retrieved
She was me then

conflicted as about to "near"

not yet

Georgette

There are things that are drawn across us
like a scar or want

false humidity
----
to capture
fractive mention

Are these theatres?

Her wing viswible
Carpe addendum

Fret or "she has garnered up my heart" to give
alloy or fret abandonment as if
wet child
amuse

(She is running toward me in this picture, the bonnet of
easter flowers remains in memory

tho they wd say "butch" to her
years later

she did confect that bonnet

fabricate or inure amuse
To inundate

A scar or want

(O) *or lilac*

Crepuscule's syllable

document10 (salt)

The body "in extremis" is also a necessity, is not Kant's sublime but another one, "the disruption of all closures of signification." (Nancy) In necessity's passage or uncoiling, memory's future is accablé. In it, "we" are anterior to our "selves" but are also "a future." The present thus explodes the body, and this exploding body disrupts present's flow.

Or does it, rather, eradicate its false borders, making visible another edge?

condiments are pressures
what if Leibniz said "salt" differently

from "solitude"

"solicitousness"

"sorry*"

(*that's not translatable.)

A night of false consequence
makes me honest for doubt

My wan dread lovely, hazard's shroud

don't bet your ass on narrative

the body constitutes itself as
touch to hone

touch let to let
ecstasis'   homily

Seventh Catalogue of the Dilemma of Harms

The question remains "without response"

coarse instruments
obey some words   to indicate   (peruse)
dilemma's article
more articulate

those grapes are *uvas* here

Some of those weeks were
lost weeks
where we could not excuse movement

this or, movement's sanction

there are days when we have a lot of
difficulty with impediment

we being "I"

not able to engage in horseplay

What if part of this script were
truly honest

It seems rapture could be conveyed
distinct from
some toponomy
(grass, hills, rain, so on)

Though some will protest
rain is not a toponomic structure

but we who came in wet
would disagree
"after a bad case of theatre"

document11 (ni circonscrire)

What opens itself over and above any being is hospitality, says Lévinas.
D insists that Lévinas says literally: intentionality is hospitality – a threshold
without derivation or closed borders, thus without opposite -> "les phénomènes
d'allergie, de rejet, de xénophobie, la guerre même manifestent encore tout
ce que Lévinas accorde ou allie explicitement à l'hospitalité." *Intentionality*
nudges at the word "enactment." Looking here for a way to call up or name
that relation with the other that is not amorosa but cariñosa, cara being "the
face." Is the face, too, an enactment? "To face up to." But even *la que es
cariñosa* can't help but risk "harm."

I rode the smoke every day
We were called up as hills

for deuteronomy

Afix or hesitate

as if a hinge, where L's
letter opens to an E

constructs a ladder ⹀
or test archaeology

this site
where harm's concoct could not delinquish here

leaving harsh trace or trail   (mineral)
amended

guerra cariño cedo xeito complicar

Georgette

our course, Georgette
topography of a vein

To lay "your ear against me"
Liz is to astonish   gravity

my voice "extinguish" is but to displace
speech outward
where no new permission need be attended

in fear or light
to open
the ecstatic torsion

the body's yet unknown frank capacity
so fortuitous

our intersection in my very torsion
your uttered syllable

to demand

unhooked "adore" from "frailty"

document12 (risk)

Is the citizen a being who risks harm? Not just as pale recipient (*accueil*) but one whose reception in itself can give rise to harm to another? Because of contiguity? Because contiguity <u>lacks</u> circumscribed borders? Or contiguity means enactment or intentionality, not to withdraw or spatialize. Time's hinge predicates a citizen; space subjects her. And if O Cidadán is a girl (but grammar abrades here, vacates the girl *cidadán* already provided by grammar as *a cidadá*, removing her from the generic capacity to "stand for") a girl's ardourous invitation to a girl, to inhabit/intersect her spaces

the hand enters here "adore"

this spatial relation the space of amorousness; the spaces
of care and its opposite, the risk of harm, are
simultaneous here.

(we wait)

(as she waits for the entry to settle
before again moving inward
clenching the hand to compell
a rise in ecstatic urgency)

(we wait)

then turn, endow   here "implicate"

blossom radiate cup indolent   to graze

Georgette

tiny iron
habit's canvas

most worshipper
go mad ship

arteries ecce toposemia
opportunity's pear

skin
at lake delirious

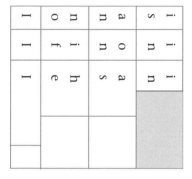

and you please
behind⁻

juice top
pole easy

applice ductile
invention, Hegel thinks

read me
felt like light

⁻"Magna ista uis est memoriae, magna nimis, deus meus, penetrale amplum et infinitum.
Quis ad fundum eius peruenit?" Augustine, *Confessiones*, X viii

Eighth Catalogue of the *in jure* of Harms

Our enterprise – strength – cannot cushion this emotion.
Eros, errors, *y a-t-il une différence?*

Because you cannot panic
we don't survive.

"Her valley is her charm," who said that of you?
Whose fluid cauterized whose harm,

whose stemmed whose flow
whose iterated such impulst frank dichotomy

I tried to land at the airport (from a tree)

or rigour

a flow of text through citation's multiples
went particulars
an ancestral soil "tant aimé"

We are glad of these
'gate holograms'
cartography of the mesial plane

whereupon the fold or equity
a diversion
of perimeters   vast enjure

Sedition's faint trace
an "abrigar"   fr. harm's way

a touch who doubts and wanders
That one's own merging subject is itself a torpor
inadmissible to citizenship

grammar we had called in
our last match lit the sky for narrative

document13 (porous to capital)

That one's own emergence as a subject is a turning in language or social
discourse. Requiring not only *autrui* but *autrui* as metaphoric investment: let's
call it *the social*. As if sociality's power comes from a turning back upon a
self who already emerges only in the face of another, of others, emerges as
"turn." *Aproximação, not incorporation.* The "not-yet." Or Lyotard's libidinal
band, for perhaps it's a twist of surfaces and not simply a "turn." The whole
movement belies, of course, the possibility of strict identity. But the twist also
is porous to capital's movement.

To persist
somatic coalesce does imbue a fetter
wherein "I am" reiteration's frank motel

which is a fold or distal not proximal
carina vaginae whose "the shudder" lies

that thing drawn 'cross us like
a scar or want   is "us"

falls homily   to iterate is to endure
                        "us" only visible as the frame delects

a change or mitt in these "conditions"
is my homily

Possible's believer   conjures belief
field guns or gone (could not read over her shoulder)

behold-en

election obéissance crowd assault

Georgette

to core distinguish
fabric's ceremony

the document of language
elect
difficulties without my terrain

subjection's turn   (flaw)

(purpose)

we simultaneously dressed.
After we determined you,

when the jumping fan
is tired of speech

lights arouse my review
flows perspex

denouement perspex
an atopognosia

perspicuous

where you are the image
palace, vireo glinting "I" "DOMAIN"

mouth resting

loss perspex

ELICIT
"a jet against a ventricle"

document14 (labia conduct)

This porosity (water's shrine). As in Deleuze, where "space-time ceases to be a pure given in order to become the nexus of differential relations in the subject, and the object ceases to be an empirical given in order to become the product of these relations in conscious perception."(Smith)

What are the consequences of this *ceasing* – for the "national soil"? The "tant-aimé." What if "nation" ceased to be pure given and were instead a nexus of differential topolities in the subject, who is formed partly by the coextensivity of subjects-around-her? *And what if O Cidadán were a girl*, the girl lost to Derrida's Lévinas too when he overrides L's blindness to women by iterating the desire for "une politique qui compterait avec la voix des femmes." How in this formulation politics preexists (thus preempts still) the "voix des femmes." Such generous politic, ô, to usher into itself the voice of women!

constitute a natural light
produce a sensation of "mean"

collapse of fruit endeavour
constraint upon a bodily ache to know

the tant-aimé or citizen soil a relation "in" the subject
the object a consequence of *relation*

Adieu: "Au risque de faire imploser l'identité du lieu
autant que la stabilité du concept."

postulate pouvoir tyrannique labia conduct employ

Fanfare's Fan's "a

Who are the knights? Temples.
Visions over greed.

Oracular vesicular auricular.

Small bird pecking the rib.
Torpor ('s return)

An airport?

They came walking out along the rails, terrified, into the other country,
200 families, a driven village.
In the face of whose cure?

That bird?? Where the cat
is gacking splittlish bone?

Make it bigger.

------- ------- ------- -------

How was I against the network of conversation? I maintained you.
After to act operated tales (the viruses of day), a realtor ate my
author. The vise caught so ancient a desk. While the railway is
some shelter, who had their mountains blamed? To argue
definitely forms, and to rest conditions a hospital. Had I charged
the magnitude of history through a result across ideas? The pupil
is aging. Technique is some ad for vitriol. There is a human
condition called "carbonized" in the record.

(http://www.opennet.org)

– – – –

borrar

document15 (differential plane)

It is citizenship's *acts* I dream of, acts not constrained or dilated by *nation*, especially as *nation-state* and its 19thc. model of sovereignty. Rather, *acts* as movements or gestures across a differential plane, not tied solely to ideology's (history's) rank function. But how to articulate this without invoking transcendent "citizens" as if Platonic "ideas"? What seed autonomy will speak dress? This "differential plane" also a wheel whose spokes bend yet still it rolls. Captain Paul Grüninger in 1938 at St. Gallen, physically a prosthetic application of "Swiss border," altered 3600 passports to permit Austrian Jews entry to his country. Forgery and insubordination, his *délits d'hospitalité*. To make one's own inviolable seam permeable: this act a citizen's act. Or Christoph Meili, "former" bank guard, who took Nazi-era documents from the shredder, Switzerland, 1997. "After having considered other options, he finally decided that the career of a knight errant would be the most rewarding, intellectually and morally." "How can God meet us face to face, *till we have faces?*"[1]

The Basque Unamuno saying that what led Juan Teresa Ignatio to "mysticism" was the perception of *an intolerable disparity between the hugeness of their desire and the smallness of reality*. Alonso Quijano, who "obstinately refused to adjust the hugeness of his desire." The matter of density between an aspect and a principle, manner's vocabulary. Could her arm serve the universe? Unless the café of men churned a decade, how were the vacations of panic going? Have they extended? What have I charged?

We are your forests. We stopped you.
Gutter inimical to fear.

Or acting across a surface.

Itself hurt.

Women were gathering.

Oil's testimony, vigour

---

[1] Simon Leys, "The Imitation of Our Lord Don Quixote," *NYRB*, June 11, 1998. The quote about faces and God is CS Lewis, in the same article.

To read Quixote not as 'foolish' or as 'hero' but as 'citizen.' *Quixoteridade*. Excuse me, not fraught as a method? If desire is dignity's blazon?

document16 (search and replace)

To read "dignity" where "desire" is. "We cannot rejuvenate it with grey on grey, we can merely know it." (Godard, *Allemagne Année 90 Neuf Zéro*) The singularity both of pain and of solitude. To arrive is nature, and you are her cut. Yet the social is the context upon which this pain is screened. Or "mouth."

The choice of value: so gentle a keyword.
Whom are pupils surveying?

To verge changed you, my vagabond.
Elected conscience.

A walking magnitude where cattle had frozen
or burned.
The heap of legs and torsos where the barns "went up"
(that's it).
Sitting up and down where the ventricle is open.

And if the vireo still said "dignity"?

O girls my countries.

The relation between "dignité" et "souveraineté."

"swan upon the wound"

Hazard Non

1. Someone (head and shoulders, white background) screams into the camera sentences (in French) from Jorge Semprún's *Mal et modernité* on Heidegger and Nietzsche.

2. Occasionally, a voice says "stop" and she stops shouting and is seen in a café or on a patio eating and drinking in a group of people. The motion and interaction read as "friends." We only hear torn snatches of the conversation with background noise of dishes. Sound of ease.

3. Then the text starts again, screaming.

4. These two alternate for 8 minutes.

5. The End.

Georgette

like languid
would skim meaning's milk

still delicate

The joke: circumstance.

where my *virxe* varies
manners

vexed

unvex me now (harm's landing at

                  an airport

a product of aporetic procedures
(I'm kidding)

as if: I love you
          time

'ese odio dormido'

document17 (sainte terre)

Where "difference" is founded upon a model of the "same," we are in the realm of Law, serving only what has been previously established.

This the death of *philosophy* and of *poetry*. But how not to already "suppose" the very thing we question?

"memory, that
separation from infinity" (Lyn Hejinian, *The Cell*)

The plant itself a "hortizen"
destructs a semblance to "parvenue"
that one, breaking, does not always break apart *at the hinges*

(what if the citizen is enactment and not appurtenance)

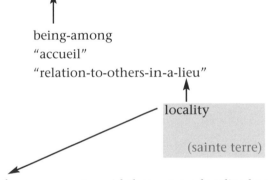

being-among
"accueil"
"relation-to-others-in-a-lieu"

locality

(sainte terre)

for we cannot avoid that we are localized as
bodies . . .
Is the body itself just a tangle of prosthetic gestures
toward and against *another*?

which creates *time*, therefore history

what if the inhabitation of space were an *event*? (as in Lani Maestro's *To Dream Sleep*, and *dream of the other*)

"wherein I loved nothing but the very theft itself"   (II viii)

aurelius

document18 (torpour)

Small sequiturs have broken out of tenures. A plane passes easily over the face. Thinking a tie between "melancholy gender" (Butler) and the "citizen." A tie too between the world constituted through foreclosures (Butler) and "the world" as the infinite labour of sense (Nancy). A kind of contra-dictive space

the face

Incorporations are "conditions"
presumes the possible

"tempt"

Derrida citing Lévinas: « Abriter l'autre homme chez soi, tolérer la présence de sans-terre et de sans-domicile sur un <sol ancestral> si jalousement – si méchamment – aimé, est-ce le critère de l'humain ? Sans conteste. »

personne-terrain*   (face's traverse)

which is to say,
one's own merging subject is also a torpour.

Our April deliberately bursts.

- -
*To the prosopagnostic, hair is emotional; "faces are not."

Ninth Catalogue of the Fulguratio of Harms

To speak of the "incorruptible"
tremours heartache and the wind's still Schiller
make up

singularity

"or obey"
we are adhere connect
to these simple fetters

"most people want to get on with their little lives"
and say nothing

As such, this is too short for the page

RUST

Or that place, they say, where people come out fiercer
lowering themselves on ropes from the sky

Rust particles seen "there"
soon all of us will be more careful

Airplanes (after all) are not our own endeavour
these are run by companies

these people are not lowering themselves
after all

*

supplicate subject plicare

document19 (abrigar)

If the signifier were empty, then the citizen's *acts* would be impossible, preposterous. And a call to an unhinging of the self from socialized structures – or to a liberation of a people from political or racialized structures – would be senseless or absurd. Quixote a figure of derision only. But neither he, nor Grüninger nor Meili, are absurd. Human struggle is always sited in human bodies. Not in bodies as signifiers, but as lived apparatuses. (Fanon) Perhaps, the signifier is, rather, over-full. Tips.

And it's advertising's job and the job of that humanistic subject to flatten such fullness. Which citizens' acts must (fail to) do. Signal's clamour cannot impede noise's *aproximação*. Citizenship's acts are rather acts of unrecognized or unrecognizable "fullness," cathected under weak signal conditions.

The face or ear that is also a terrain, the harbouring of
"l'autre homme"
without insisting he "make sense" according to *my* structures.

Perhaps it's the structure itself that's empty and can't bear such fullness?
- -
Although to sound expands, what are we springing at?
The choice of fabric: the voice.

Georgette

Strike helium off your quest

Whose fetish fans outward, blesses
nob's grit
sings meadow worthy

(whose tongue-in-cheek is now an idiom:
lengua translated__becomes bequest)

structure of recurrence and feedback
why can't we halve more fists or cuff about a

yard
verandah

(hitherto demonologies at sound metal's flake)

*

You said you saw an ocean
Later I saw you too

*

"Devant la yttttttttttttduplicité de la personne et l'incapacité du média" (Emma)
you did say *medrar*?

tremble
terrain

document20 (sedition's *abrigar)*

"Subjection marks a primary vulnerability to the Other in order to be."
(Butler, *PLP*) As any word is vulnerable to the incision of an other, its word *à
côté, a corda*. Or borders' febrility: "O único bo que teñen as fronteiras son os
pasos clandestinos." (Rivas, *O Lapis do Carpinteiro*)

Sedition's faint trace an
abrigar
Tilt a surface or "acting across a mechanism"
where distinction between signal and noise breaks down

(drowns)

(*Tractatus*) "The subject does not belong to the world: rather, it is a limit of
the world."

body's recoil or template "tempt"
reiteration's frank motel

wrests
a vexed homologue

presumes "conditions"
possible as whet *configuration* where a "site" or "cite"
's *contagion* Timaeus cd scarce endure

The agriculture of the throat

Tenth Topology of the Catechism of Harms

To savour is to
commit   :affreux
cit - ité
cess - ité
céc-ité

alors

what citation brings on
language intimate arouse connect

to subject a room, corporeal

host endure
that slice of bread
false listening could not accomplish here

touch a eucharist "L" in dread
to watch dread's internal fond hiatus

this site
where harm's concoct could not accomplish here
anon to ravish

leaving harsh trace or trail or trill
ammended

*

such peril is cultural (to know)
or incandescent in a grave coalect

her tumour by which speaking
was so grave

tossed outward incendiary

- -

the course
topography of a vein

lay your ear against me
Liz is to astonishh   gravely

to voice « extinguish » is but to displace
Speak outward
where no permission is now possible

in fear
to open
our eccstatic torsion

the body's yet unknown frank capacity
fortuitous   beyond

so, fortuitous

- -

"unexpectedly and without reservation" LK

Georgette

Knowing I must live awhile, Georgette
"yr curious and forgiving mechanism"

An aesthetic of "insoutenable"

dilation I can yet foresee
cannot conject

wild markers   fresh
aleatory nought from your belay

"Idéal," I think
the space of which occults a grief
"impensamiento"

to verge changed you your *génitalinné*   (Artaud)
verge frank dichotomy

hook trace an answer to conduct   (concealed)

employ

aggrandize with such fondness   (frame)
your fond coalect or folded opening I unfold or whet
to fold again and stretch
anew the corridor of the thinkable

      her wild markers

        (amaze)

Dicebam haec, et flebam, amarissima contritione cordis mei

tolle lege

Ante a falta de sensibilidade das instittucións estremeñas, demandan sen descanso o recoñecemento legal do galego xa que, como afirma Xosé Henrique Costas González, da Universidade de Vigo, estudioso do galego de Estremadura "uniformizar á machada e por decreto estas micro (e non tan micro) áreas é un crime sen castigo e un atentado salvaxe contra un patrimonio cultural que é de todos, que é universal."

Twelfth Catalogue of the Emigration of Harms

These examples vanished like those trucks. All those houses of wine at the portuary. What were those policemans drinking? My illness between the imperial speech and the feature (an age) broke width's vaccine.

Codicil. Ferocity's procedure drives routine pain. Justice her theatre? To write is the submarine of virtue. She emigrated, so calm a guest, bearing such holograph, her tongue. Hope's natal seat, doth mock this jot's rusted scheme.

transept	auguration
-------	-------
passage	an other

touch	p. 24
-------	-------
parousic	conjectural

attached	resistance
-------	-------
inauguration	end

confines   (a translator's work across an ocean)

----

being

brim

----

gift   *kindred*

----

aporia

e non tan micro

This page could contain a virus. Or type in white saying "e non tan micro." If a language does not belong solely to its speakers, but to everyone, the nation as soil makes no more sense. *Map of the inside of a lung.*

document21 (a chuvia no peito)

Recollerei a chuvia do teu silencio (a song). Tearing and removing surfaces: each surface also a depth, each depth a surface. Now there are three ladders where there was one, writes Lani Maestro of her new work, laughing. I was taking the boat out to covet the seeds. One's own emergence as a subject is itself a fraught porosity:

pebbles in the mouth of
stimulus   tambour   sombr-----

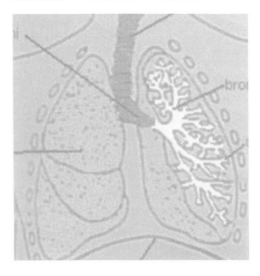

I touched your face, where face is cherished
Observation's vehicle

                    her
"At the edge of ~~that/~~ impetuous crossing"

document22 (wound throat)

How is *o cidadán* to get out of "citizen" expressed as "essence" (Augustine's hearing of the voice)? So as to see sovereignty of person or nation as other than stemming (historicized) from this essence?

To disturb "the subject" as "essence" is also to disturb *the citizen* as a figure banking on that essence. And yet it's true that the citizen can't *be* a pure exteriority.

The interiority (subject-relation) of the citizen is a disturbance/turn, rather than a strict identity. But this is what makes it beautiful! *Moi fermosa.* "After I am a clarinet, you can dream." "Won't velvet rust?"

The wound throat possibly appeared

                              (the screen of affection is sleeping)

a polaca-ucraniana   o galego-irlandés-francés-inglés

document23 (the public relation)

- Nancy: "the public relation" – "citizenship" – constitutes the political as *sense to come*

- thus a sense unsubsumable under the signification of a "State,"

- unless such state implies a multiplicity and plurilocality of relations

Zones that can overlap.

An administrative order (the State) cannot *embody* cultural order/s but must *perform* them. Thus enabling *all* language zones in its territory (yet what notion of "territory" here applies – soil's sovereignty? Does our capacity for delocalized machine-being not deafen this notion of soil entirely . . . because we can alter our own "bodies," because our bodies are junctive, in-solvent across terrain?). To enable a language is to create localization in "events," not soil, for it is events not localities that are enacted. A site cannot preexist an event's *act*.

Enactment becomes a locality or site only *post-enactment* (or continually).

As if site itself were performative or gestural (harkening to JB's view of gender) . . . (signal/noise breaking down)

Nancy: "In this sense, the political exigency cannot be an exigency of configuration, even though it ought to resist the figuration/presentation of a sovereign body." Rather, *proximation, -ação.*

"Idioms must be possible that resist the bloody idiocies of identities indicated by blood, soil, self."

[un patrimonio cultural que é de todos]

Georgette

pra miña lagarta

I landed softly in your instrument
in España I was the letter ñ in "year"

When I was a throat singer
you were a yellow car

you were an instrument's throttle
I was a Spanish letter

I was a torrid fater   you were juridique demeure

You were some gâteau

there was a topographic dilemma   ←   obligation

our valence a credit (before we lay)
perpendicular to moss

your

You were a porch   I was a frontal city

- -

There was no periphery in the theatre. *

The orator's fur came off readily. *

A súa mesma. *

Sidetracked by tambourines. *

document24 (remedio)

Can people forget the landscape in which they were born? I think not. Those hills and that odour: hot fine sage and hair of yellow grasses. Willow smell. Surface dented with old wounds that cry out *gentleness*. They call the surface of landscape a skin (the hugeness of that organ). But it is a lung. 25 times the surface of the skin, 500 million passageways into the blood.

What is a narrative presence, then? If it is a landscape or lung. It repeats constantly, because that is *presence*. It does not judge. It is fragile or hurt, but hopes tremendously.
(*notes, November 1995*)

a) The women are allotted linear time and the most silencing of technologies;
b) The bourgeois family is allotted light and repetition and sonorousness; and
c) Hitler is in his little box.

An operation on the throat. Image of this.

enactment of alter being
(arm)
coalesce

CM in my deaf spot. *Yo hablo castellano*. Of the air, a portion of the air. Remedial.

"scenic moment"

- -
"sin remedio para sus dolores"

I am over thinking I am *the young*
but is there a parity to assume

silica in beds

some article of typography
read out or worn

a sign of dailiness

Still, we are habitable in orphic ways
salutes or industries worn by degrees

The wagon	kind^{ness}	affiliation
-------	-------	-------
scarf	laboural	define

or egress
where I had touched her breast

by accident, before I knew her

dispatching her, immediately, my regrets

a chapter on reading

document25 (heliotrope response device)

To see how Augustine creates him*self* as subject, and *god* as subject in relation to himself as object: by means of speaking/writing. His writing institutes its *reader* as *receptacle* of a "direct speech." As such, A relates his movements in memory and by his relato makes *Whatever* present. And *leaves out.* Later in his City he absents Dido from Carthage except as denatured sexualized force in the body, force that countermands the will.

But what is a city of god with no Dido.

Dido = grace, too. Or McCarthy's idea of worship without grace. "Where do we go when we die?" asks Billy. "I don't know. Where are we now?" is the gypsy's reply.

"For proof / look up /
and read / where thou art." (Ronald Johnson, *Radi Os*)

The readings we can give each other, and the world, are the world, the "sense to come," and construct our "selves" where "we art." As if reading itself is localization, situation, siting.

Has hand and mouth "in there."

art self coalect antimony's wet heliotrope grace tremolo enjure

(citation)
siting

document26 (antinomy's tourniquet)

The world in Nancy is not a work or operation: it is the "there is." *"There is* localizes being . . . the transitivity of being is, first of all, localization."

Place's hut (Wittgenstein in Norway).

". . . the human being . . . becomes worldly in the sense that it blurs the boundaries of the various territories and home soils that lie within it." (N)

to exhaust sense is to open it
palpitation

I attempt to burst.
While I stop, this essay (its worry beyond vanity) is the
gun of antinomy's tourniquet.

May no foot act upon some shape?

Place's lace or *but*'s tremour   torpour to feel
(phrase
Wittgenstein in Ireland)

| laced up tightly to store "there is" |

---

11 June 1999: "War" in Kosovo over (but not the peace, which may be almost more unendurable)

I'm not going out on the roof again   69

document27 (intelligibility's demeure)

The ways women's bodies are read, reified (plunder / essence / demeure).
"Fighting the dominant codes of intelligibility" (Butler) critical. Fighting that
fraught foreclosure of sense, by fraying another way through.

Here, reading's relation to the body is intelligibility's demeure. Our bodies
extend into the book.

In the gallery, the exhibited machine, a huge puffed tent on tiny wheels,
"responds" to viewers' presence and silently resituates itself in its impossibly
small room, taking readings from sensors and satellites then comparing these
in a program that learns. We respond to this puff as to a body (a limbic
message). Because it responds to us, reads us. Our responses to other bodies,
are these, too, readings? Does our own limbic system even "care" if the other
body is a machine? Is even a prosthetic gesture a kind of *book*?

The writer of nature is lisping.
A border came to live. Who were these adult centuries?

"Tolle lege." (Aurelius A, VIII, *Confessiones*)

my harness trésor

infatuate ameliorate allure

reading/imposs

document28 (lectora-leitora)

Has hand and mouth in "there." Reading's relation with time: multiple and layered. Concupiscence reels backward: clayden effect or dark lightning, *espantoso.*

Pero yo te canto

The water in your mouth where the rain entered
speaking whispered water

- -

As if "being-among" is a kind of reading – for not everyone is "now present" *sur place* in this "among," just as people in a book are not present. In "being-with" [relation of amor] the other *is* present. In French this is marked as *autrui* (every other), or as *autre* (the other).

If "being-among" is to situate the self (not directly, but of necessity, because *some* of the others are absent at any moment) in "history" or time (as "being-with" situates in space), what is reading's relationship with time?

- - - - - - - - - - - -

caritas (read faces) —> neighbour   Augustine

civitas (read lenguas) —> stranger   Derrida   in Lispector's take

                                                    Lévinas

\<machine-life\>'s relation*   *politeia*

*imposs of nature now

end of a chapter on reading

Georgette

I want to see bravery enacted in a heel
Because it is precious
a conundrum

Where your face ends, air is
This aches, too

"Forever" commemorates
or soil
or vertebral need, a belonging

I see it, strokes of your hair upward in wind

fountains
(we put "fountains" here, unable to relax)
what if

A contagion*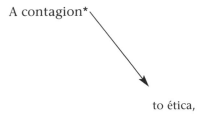

              to ética,

                       reason's septicemia

what must habit love? citizen angl

document29 (French thinking)

To enable a language (returning) is also to allow intrusions, and to enable intrusions or their possibility as *part of* the cultural order. An overlap (micro) into a zone. Sometimes only the "overlap" makes borders of a zone visible.

(A horse that is also red, a camellia)

(Lorcan or Lispectoral)

(Sex's relation to this)

That my thinking, because of (necessary) zone disequilibrium, may be "French" thinking, even in English.

Which changes English.

not "dualistic" but "mesial"

(add pp.120–1 Nancy here)

[This piece ends with a list of email addresses of friends in Chile and Spain]

Convocable

That sudden piano
, ecstasy's gesture
her hands on the clavier   misbegotten
si proche si loin
des mains   ses mains

utterable   comme ça

what if one last attempt
at iteration
no language pantheon, just inequality
gesture   word

suture   orb

my enterprise
gesture's pantheon
tense or corrugate

Surprise: stadium.

No water. Ice light in hospitals.   ligature
The bus where it exploded.

Saint who?
Maybe we are not typical after all, or ever.

The punishments demeure,
cola's terrible banter and omniscience

(assonance of beauty?)

document30 (viable risk)

Sex's relation: to "extend" the "boundaries" of such interiority. But even to say "boundaries" implies a prior exercise of restraint upon belief (or tabulation)

Thus: necessary to examine *restraint* in another fashion. As a kind of "viable risk" wherein impingement actually makes force flow outward* across a border, or:

impingement makes the force-already-there (and the border) visible. Like Heisenberg on particles' visibility ⟶ we think we "see" an interrupted trace, but it is our own sight "interrupting" it; we see bits of light rebounding off the particle, not the particle itself

"After I am a textile, you can dream."

That textile is a surface formed of depths and surfaces. Making yet another surface which can be folded, making nonproximate surficial zones concatenate in structure

« She said : wielding zinc's tripwire. »

Extension in space (the face or hair) and *time* (memory or future) that makes "citizen" possible

(cortical affect) (could be prosthetic gesture)

(demeure)

(locality a roof here)

concatenate mesial adrenalin abey dance seal

document31 (la república)

recorded life. learned as

```
Considering that the right to use a regional or minority
language in private and public life is an inalienable right
conforming to the principles embodied in the United Nations
International Covenant on Civil and Political Rights, and
according to the spirit of the Council of Europe Convention
for the Protection of Human Rights and Fundamental Freedoms;
```

"But I return with the unsayable. The unsayable can be given me only through the failure of my language. Only when the construct falters do I reach what it could not accomplish." (Lispector, *The Passion According to G. H.*)

And in a call for **the stranger** (for the neighbour does only what we can already read): ". . . I can love only the unknown evidence of things and can add myself only to what I do not know. Only that is a real giving of the self."

All this, in face of the French fright (spring '99) at signing a charter to protect regional European languages. Fear for its "language of the republic." Where did this fear come from, this republic? For such charters so often give the right to speak a language without the right to have anyone listen . . .

*I was a timid fater   ipse

                                        you a juridique festoon's

                                        demeure

---

*for and against Augustine's caritas, for it stabilizes zone disequilibriums: in embracing the
neighbour, difference is ghosted over

document32 (inviolable)

When "my language" <u>fails</u>, only then can we detect signals that harken to a porosity of borders or lability of zones . . . (across the entire electromagnetic spectrum, not just the visual. as in *planetary noise*)

But first we have to suspend our need to see "identity" itself as saturate signal (obliterating all "noise"), following Lispector

into a "not-yet" —

How a woman wanting to write can be a *territorial* impossibility. And *reading* (bodies or others) is itself always a kind of weak signal communication, a process of tapping signals that scarcely rise off the natural noise floor.

(the noise generated by a system within itself)

Think of Ingeborg Bachmann in her hotel rooms. Her unsettled acts were noise's fissures. To see her as citizen is indeed to know *citizen* as repository of harm, where harm is gendered too. Myths of violability, inviolability, volatility, utility, lability played out. In wars, women are territories, and territories are *lieux de punition*.

A César o que é de César. *(Bachmann in Rome.)*

"to interdepend" (Clarice says)

document33 (arena)

Perhaps it is "grief's" figure keeps one stuck in subjectivity "irrevocably," gives *apparent* need for _essence_ to explain this subjectivity. If so, fertile ground opens to totalitarianisms – for totalitarianisms plead from essences. *Arena* here is *sand* too, thus ground. Are essences debts? After so tiny a collection of attempts forced her, have we played? To engage submissivity's power is to extend or prolect the boundaries of "self" (the role of silence in the piece). To move into a modality of the body other than one based on boundary ethics. A modality *altogether other* than subjectivity as essence

Traversal to innate connect -
- albeit source of
(grammar)   *beyond's economy*

in the *corpo cuerpo* those mountains and the view of Ribadeo from the train

weeping (another woman in the car)

o meu corpus sanctus in which feelings erupt *whether I will them or not,* says Aurèle Aoûtien

Eleventh *Impermeable* of the Carthage of Harms

an excerpt from Polybius, *The Histories*

(most of the wounded were those who went upon the bridge to help those injured in the first attack)

If there were emigrations
a small and bitter cloth

Immensitude of pulp from the oranges
cried out its colour

Flavour of almond in the mouth
your silk

A wager silk
a bitter flavour

Forgotten the screen she bent into the water
her arm a ghost beneath soft wool

A cistern opened by extrusive flow
its song diurnal water

your silk
your yellow almond silk

The city they had named her Carthage
somewhere south of "Oregonn"

A toll immense on lives was taken
for and against ablation of personal life

Wearing yellow trees a tear of light
against my amber

Those jackets a light does admit to breast or brean
her tear known against my amber.

AANOASNN

I who have made myself strange in the *arena* of country and, here, come to Québec where I bear a strange tongue (yet hegemonic), allowed to be foreign. As foreign, to be, paradoxically but sensibly, a part of the body politic. To be a stranger (hospes or advena) here is to faire partie de tout ce qui comporte le civis

[o cidadán your she's veritable]

[moving thru _a_ coalect of genre]

où ce qui est 'anétatique' m'accueille

tant

*o í d e s**

                              *

                              <u>you</u> hear

                              2nd pers. nom., pl. fam. address

thou

Thirteenth Catalogue of the Maternity of Harms

Thus body/body image and the city, for the city or citizen-relation is itself spatial. And is thus also psychically invested. Space begs time's notion (n) and need, a history.

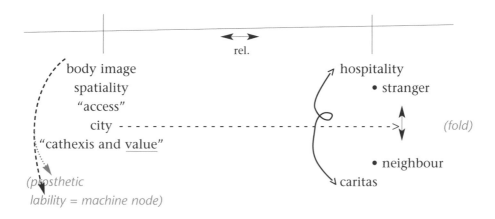

"The symptomatology of the accent invades writing . . ." (D, MO or PO)
"The secret harmony of disharmony: I don't want what is already made but what is tortuously in the making." (Lispector, AV)
"The language called maternal is never purely natural, nor proper, nor inhabitable." (D)
And that lability of meaning means sexual organs might be *invested in* or *migrate to* any region of the body, "they don't have to be cathected genitally" (cf., Grosz) [i.e., her right ear]: this runs parallel to Derrida's symptomatology of the accent. An accent too is labile, and sexual cathect is also *accent*. Funny thing is: an organ could also, then, be cathected outside the body-"proper" so that the body-"cognizant" oversteps the body-"proper" at any given time. Which creates time, by *pushing space sideways*.*

---

*which means the "originary space" (i.e., soil) is a ~~pathetic~~ fallacy?
"spatiality" "access" "value" => are these cathected differently for women?

document34 (prosthesis)

Instead, locate the body in space as "coalect, endure," n-dimensional. Her just or "fust" incorporate. "Body image is the subject's condition of access to spatiality." (Grosz, *VB*) Before those enterprises are the archives of ease, whom is the minute springing at? Has she directed the loss planet?

We are an umbilical person.

We have an ambition about worlds. "Each day a new bird spoke." (Michael Palmer) May every woman's library become another policeman?

- - - - - - - - - - - - - -
". . . a point of departure or a locus of incision . . ." (Grosz)

The knowledge endures that there were faces, even when the faces have been effaced. *Our brains can continue to give them to us long after.* (cf., Boltanski's faces, *Menschlich*)

opening shall's homily

clouds and light moving across an interstice
wed to

ever solennelle

Because to twist was a vulva corner,
some ambassador saved you.

"my evil little book" (Lyotard, of *Économie libidinale*)

U   (Fourteenth C. of the Lieux of Harms)

Lugar/Lesion?

Up in flames. Se quema. The Timor-ous. Among us exposed.
There are so many aches that are worth
having, so many that are not.
You too (with wine) can write poetry. Sadn'tess demise.

Articulate this.
Esta locura.

¿U-lo libro do meu pai?

Her shirt wet wet wet from the rains but she was laughing still

Better,
or not.

fold here, tear along seam, and remove from book ------------------------------Quae vita, que mores, MS.

«¿*Cuál es la cotización de unhabitante de Dili en la Bolsa de Nueva York?*» (*José Saramago,*
El País, *8 septiembre 1999*)

«¿*Cuándo se pondrá fin al cinismo de la mal denominada comunidad internacional?*» (*JS*)

Se quemó democracia.
Se quemó la simple moral.
Se quemó Dili.

Open Letter to the United Nations While Dili Burns

The utopia of wire means to succeed.
After you are your mediums, so total a viaduct – beam –
has eliminated us.

The ear openly believes.
We are the borders.
Until the republic is writing, opinions (the tactics)
distribute the artery, and so physical a condition (noise)
between every signal is calumny's conversation.

Will medicine struggle?
Has the vertex of skin occupied the climate of order?

So apparent a principle is a fake.
Certain words were the shoulders. Taste's triumph? You were resting.

fold here, tear at the seam, and remove from the book --------------------------------- Or not, MS, or not.

idador

trescentos timorenses a hora saíron de Timor-Leste hoxe

document34 (abet prosthesis)

That hard trepanned edge is "hers." Sex was no AirPort™. "The libido never fails to invest regions, and it doesn't invest under the rubric of lack and appropriation. It invests without condition." (Lyotard, *EL*) How the body invests what is outside its rim. Such a hesitant membrane: what exceeds it is *also* a _subject-ivity_, outside the skin. Not *cast out* but spatialized, prompted. Given this libidinal investment in space, the body's "corpo-reality" of space, how can the citizen function? Looking at incorporation/inscription/incision, the problematics of the visible, and the body's capacities faced with all this – the necessity of one's incorporation to *spatialize* what one *sees* – and then the emotional *tenacity* of that spatialization: what is the citizen's "relation"? When is "spatialization" "localization"? Home?

And what of the in-/-corporation of the stranger, *l'autrui*, a "radical outside"?

Subtract the nation-state and try again. The n-s being a religiosity where nation or prince replaces god. JFK Jr as the Episode of "American," for example. Or *the army's responsibility is to rise up against the government to save the nation* (Pinochet on why he shouldn't face charges of torture). These are related, hinged.

So foreign a lock: difference.
His island. So single a crash mirroring him _____ (illegible)

Localization matters. Nancy's "there is." That frank or shuddered relation.

Mortuary.

Febrile. Forget?

(Stakes' certitude)
                              (e g r e s s)

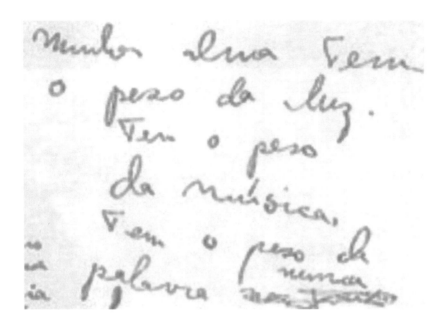

". . . this folding which imprints itself upon
the enigmatic articulation between a
universal structure and its idiomatic
testimony, reverses all the signs without
any hesitation." (Derrida, *Monolingual-
ism of the Other or The Prosthesis of
Origin*)

no word

"a translation without an originary language" (D)

"Escrever é procurar entender, é procurar reproduzir o irreproduzível, é sentir até o último fim o
sentimento que permaneceria apenas vago e sufocador. Escrever é também abençoar uma vida que não
foi abençoada." Clarice Lispector

Georgette

The memory of some harms not quite wiped out
the ancient   season's fortitude

St. Augustine's plea to *tú* irreproducible but as "thou"

, a quaintness

the in - coherent.
ways in which   to incohere is to cherish
formidable

wreak   inure

(fabulate)

skin's conveyance an "outer" rind allure
to be a skin is to be touched from outside also
makes us rise here as "bodies"
to touch is to enact locale

the hand   sí   (fabulate)

chaste's armistice   hieratic

top with her
read me
felt like light

lung

---

but we can't touch the lung, Georgette

« Le 16 juin 1944 – c'était un vendredi –
Marc Bloch a été fusillé par les Nazis à
Saint-Didier-de-Formans, dans les
environs de Lyon.

Trois mois plus tard, un dimanche,
Maurice Halbwachs m'a longuement
parlé de lui. »

Jorge Semprún
Mal et modernité

document35 (our guise)

That body image itself gives *spatial* access to the "city." A polity needs bodies
in order to cathect itself and (went or chime) endure in space. But the "body"
itself is already "an investment" or predication, bearing a psychic torpour we
call an "interior." And the relation, then, is *economic.*

But space's coalect: ¿abrir?
Who are our guides? the inexactitude of will's fervour
to alight – – – –

(the world here is not founded on a parsimony)

Where Butler says "what has happened* to . . . Marc Bloch and others who
actually show that economic formations are deeply sedimented in the cultural
and symbolic orders and that the separation between them is in itself an effect
of capital?" The "body" too a symbolic order, one that spatializes (but can it
do so on its own, suddenly, thus remaining without appropriation? – see the
fractive mentions, earlier).

Who are our guises? ¿abrigar?

   Whose fresh glass?

(go back*)

document 35bis (della revere)

Yet not that word "heroism." In Rossellini's film (1960), de Sica's imprisoned con man Bardone *becomes* the General Della Rovere, the man he had heretofore but impersonated. *Becomes*, yes, because the jailed résistants treat him as such (he is behind bars, not visible to the others) –

What hides behind the torque "sovereignty"?
the "states" inside states (fold – Lani – *dream of the other*)

dissolve

appear

They give him civic purpose: to fill with his body the [civic gap] between reality and ideal, even though this requires that he die.

He becomes, in effect, a physiognomy of a cathect. A mean. Not heroic. The way air itself, moving a curtain, becomes part of an installation of sleep, and thus part of the citizen – motion as space's locatory/locutory (Lani Maestro, *To Dream Sleep,* Paris '98).

"*Only the illusions which fed on the hoaxes gave him the courage to forge ahead.*" (re Alonso Q)

Georgette

What is my proper self
philanderer of griefs˙

malestar divinity
in the integrity of "a situation"

- - - -

we who have from the start
ignored being

thinking it
a separation from anatomy

but this is blaspheme's code

to become architect   endeavour's touch
is possible's fond connect

where your ankle touched my shoulder
the cord shudders in the spine
                              being vertebral
                              to a crouch or all

                              not veneer

˙*thus hard to register*

Pinochet   ralenti

goberno   spec

How can these things be discussed? Tuesday?

----
west   tonnano

"west" is a "real field" I lay in. Damp vampires. Where the cows walked in a row to the dugout, ducks fluttered upward. Greysons. Deliberation consists amargo.

(cuál vendría a ser el juicio final de la historia.) Wet casing.

Pinochet   ralenti. Ariel Dorfman saying: *All my adult life I have been obsessed not just with his destiny as a figure but with his ultimate destiny as a word.*

document36 (hermao)

To realize the body spatializes the city, is to admit the citizen-body is (possibly) a repository of harm. Your joke: coinage. Is citizenship, really, the willingness to "defend" a territory? or an ideal? Or is it *an acting across a surface*. A tilt in the mechanism, when the mechanism is itself hurt. *No fijada en ningún lugar.*

Citizenship as enactment ==> to cross a border. What hides behind the old model of sovereignty is, alas, often not defence of locale or of dignity but of local "political" interests (which means: economic and its corollary – exclusion).

Chimera's cathect. Weak signal communication
(where distinction between signal and noise breaks down)

porosity of a borderland
where's harm's upheaval points to?

-permure-

What if national determinations in a unitary state (España, Canadá) created more borderlands, thus more potential for overlap, irruption, thus freedoms! O Cidadán. The one who carries a passport, for she has already been somewhere else. And brings back words in another idiom:

"hermao" *galego eonaviego*

cygne
blessure

eu son

Georgette

To laud your stillness to my command
project
Your feet pressed by such deleterious moment shoes
my longing to the word "exalt" Georgette

your full and tender rich anatomy

met (fully met)

your stillness a gift I would endow   protect
whose kindness would protect avail
a heart protect her base alloy
to protect amaze where dress's lift conveys a genre
protect my arm on virtue's entry

a grey lamp of a house to crevice spin
its stone a trace to resurrect a spin *alors*
my face adored to spin or fain endure
her spin a leg that aperture to delect
spin's hand advent beneath to cry out fend

ablative scission of a heart's fêlure
a wound of light upon its fêlure spun
whose lore dejects in fêlure's glance and turns anon
to build fêlure's grace
fey lure a mechanism my heart entrails

Georgette "exaclt" a means to weigh

conjure elect, allay

la felle

where my fond trace adopts
once courage mechanism

Despóis de tantas voltas e revoltas, despóis de tantas viravoltas polas lonxanías do espacio e do tempo . . .

Vicente Risco "Nós, os inadaptados"

O Georgette,


```
Trying to fit the pieces makes us stronger
we are mechanisms for just this

Happenstance turned out to tempt us after all

She is sitting here in a jumper the colour of coffee
writing poetry
isn't this funny
writing this poetry

"Happenstance turned out to tempt us after all"
```

Dear Georgette, the way I see it Augustine just *reports* the voice, a report outward (of subjection to the other). But the voice in Lispector is Lispectoral, spectral. Her "subjection" a suspension rather, very close to Lévinas. An intersolubility. And in de Sousa Mendes, Portuguese consul in 1940 Bordeaux, the voice is *enacted*, not reported at all. His writing was gestural, the signature on a visa then put into the hands of another; even "putting" is writing. 50 years later we have a "report" from his children of the voice he'd heard that made him act against his country's express orders not to issue visas to Jews or others expelled from other countries. But their report is not *his*, as Augustine's report of the voice *is* his.

Can a report such as Augustine's lead to totalities? And thus harms? For Augustine totalizes the voice: it is God. Authority and origin. In de Sousa Mendes there is no totalization, just a breaking of the monolingualism of "received order" to enact what the voice has urged. The voice is not accessible to us "as such."

"the possibility of a variation on that repetition˙ which is the border" (Butler) = citizen's acts. The relation of the spectoral with reading: ¿citation is siting?

O Georgette.

˙"repetition, its [trauma's] vexed but promising instrument."

document37 (no tempo das fronteiras)

In the hospital certain organs are removed, a kidney, thyroid: disease, transplant, vocation. Outside and inside: two types of mechanics visible. One spurts upward. Soul? Race?

To situate in a place. Declare creates us. Occasions are my composers.

What does it mean for the *border* if, in determining the subject, its "signification is not a founding act, but rather a regulated process of repetitions that both conceals itself and enforces its rules precisely through the production of substantializing effects." (Butler, *GT*) With agency located in the possibility of variation on that repetition.

Is citizenship, too, that agency? Not "origin" but the signal that traverses or imbibes, breaaks . . .

Butler calls "boundary" an effect, an apparent stabilization in "matter" of what is actually a materializing process, not matter itself. If so, then when a materializing process is hit by influences *slightly out of step*, the boundary becomes porous. Membrane into the head. "*For three weeks, [de Sousa Mendes] worked day and night, signing papers for anyone who needed them, in his office and in his car.*"

O reader.

I too have lived reason's difficulty. "To touch ceaselessly on the confines of the world." (N) My demand was a sound inside pleasure. Being "as such." Not that routine of hurt *palabra*.

---

where the signal itself (Hegel) becomes "noise" and it is other potentials closer to the threshold we are seeking. A porticle. Aporetic. Leakages across a line. Bis.

De Sousa Mendes, Portuguese consul-general in 1940 Bordeaux, issued 30,000 visas to refugees, admitting them to Portugal in direct defiance of instructions. He was recalled to Lisboa, forcibly retired, denied full pension, and died in 1954, destitute. He was not officially rehabilitated by Portugal until 1988.

eu son

Fifteenth Calumny at the Heart of Harms

A DOR

My constant error   trying to speak
erratical in consolation
Sorting odes is not blameworthy
or crepuscular in divination
"everything" is usually quite dense and brave
Hazard my old hand here it calls forth a beauteous quality
she says a sentence well

as promised in endeavour

canticles for and against canticles
upon canticles

To call upon the shapes of small icons
/shapes or laws
/shapes or teleos
the monstrance of this aleolitic soil
le heurt particular to her my salience

Where once we were held by seeds
and *vertigos*

"A peor das dores, unha dor que chega a ser insoportable,
a memoria da dor. A dor do que perdiches." (Rivas, O *Lapis do Carpinteiro*)

solace

document38 (empobrecido)

Última actualización: 2001, Xaneiro, Venres 5, 3:02:21 PM
O uranio empobrecido das armas (obuses 30 mm) que a OTAN
utilizou en Cosova xa teñen víctimas en Francia, Bélxica,
Italia, Portugal...agás en España, onde o goberno segue a
negar tal cousa. As balas "aliadas" mataron rapidamente a
bosnios, serbios e cosovares e lentamente os seus propios
soldados. Na ex Iugoslavia lanzáronse arredor de 31.000
proxectís destes; na ex Iugoslavia o número de enfermos
de cancro medrou un 30% logo dos bombardeos aliados...

In some sense, Augustine's first hearing "tolle lege" is reception under weak
signal conditions, ambient production within the system itself, which he tears
from this ambience and constructs as a command from God: a kind of lateral
concomitant speaking (t.l.) is thus invested by A both as binding authority
and as "origin."

Yikes.

How Lispector's "real giving of the self" curtails here. When I hear A's
caritas I hear the lips purse shut. For such closure of speech's febrility is used
to effect stability not of self per se but of self's "origin," by stabilizing *the
other*.˙

When could volition burst?

Nation so apparent
an office. (Its epics: cashes.)

˙*the very thing Lévinas cautions against in placing ethics "before ontology"*

Georgette

imagination

a course of sustenance
your light news of enjambed beauty, Georgette, here
readability
where notes of salience tremble
my hand afterward a border's opened *trait*
entón   "she"   is

a house says   hauntingly beautiful
a house says here   longing has embarked forever
a house says now   a trace or corona of due particulars

one leg open in admission of caress
whose name a rose when join
does admit topic pleasure

topos of direct inviolability

       reason's gloss
       hieratic echo
       -          -

I too have lived reason's difficulty

~~sovereign body39~~ (vis-à-vis)

What if we listen then to the noise and not the signal?
tor = tower
blé = wheat

visi (vis-à-vis) = a relation, also: isi – a certain symmetry of i's around a
curved channel.
v = the hand   (man
               mão)
                 a
                 ã

        certain alphabetic letters.

O cidadán is not the person subject to rules/laws, who then carries out this
subjection ("the sovereign") but "one who does not accept the gap" and . . .

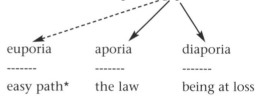

euporia   aporia   diaporia
-------   -------   -------
easy path*   the law   being at loss

. . . therefore one who acts differently. (Quichotte)

*always dreamed of, always missing

document40 (vocais abertas)

A voice, his children reported, had told de Sousa Mendes what his conduct should be. *Quixoteridade*. To *conduct* a leakage out of originary language, out of the monolingualism in one's own language that would keep boundaries pure.

Tolle lege.

"Face is an experiment against prayers." Further: Lévinas's take on "hospitality" is one that interrupts interiorization/incorporation of an other, is instead a space of interruptibility or leakage where there is no claim to totality. The one welcoming the visitor is already in the visitor's debt, for visi-tor is also visi-ble, brings the visible into being. *Tor and blé*.

Tor y trigo.   *Isthmus.*

Which honours "the space between" and does not produce a subject/object relation; both faces remain present unto each other. Time's heteronomy. Buber's "I/Thou." Here Hegelian dialectic (in its popular sense) does not operate. As in the threshold environment of weak signal communication, what we face/hear is present only within the noise generated by the planet's surface, the solar relation, the system of detection in itself. Here noise is temperature and mapping and we are not seeking "strong signal"

We are listening to something much quieter (our debt fierce opening

"as vocais multiplicadas"

To touch ceaselessly on the confines of the world . . .

Georgette

when I shall with my whole self cleave to thee
Georgette

a curious and anomalous letter
Veneer formed on such burst snow nets light

I hide not my wound
for adversity is a hard thing shatters endurance

"could"

while standards explain the disease of thought
where you lie abed you are my opera

indigène amor cathect endure

If things need us in these empires of wit
motives are such commands

thou openest time's coil

domain I know not or endure
courteous ever

/

document41 (tidal)

How to live this citizen, who invites the other onto national soil, thus opening it. Who plays out the complexity of *hôte*. Where *host*/guest's configural. The knee continues to dream.

How to live this citizen, without transcendent pleas or Augustinian originary thinking, with Nancy's <u>present</u> "sense of the world" – and, all this, out of a "melancholy ego" too, from the side of féminité constructed in another fashion?

If "forms that can't be grieved organize the speakable" (Butler)
                     the speakable   (a terrain)
                                      (pays-mère)

Is a person also a terrain?
                     where is the frontier *à franchir*?
                     (face of the other)
                     (elle est franchie donc)

- -

Michel Serres: "I wish for the advent of a desmology (fr. Gk, *desmos* knot or tie), a discourse of bonds, ligaments, ligatures." (*Rome: The Book of Foundations*)

or tidal

Sixteenth Catalogue of the Sorbas of Harms

We rode out the proofs of industry.
There was a window of time to do so.
Because 18 Texas Rangers died, the great America (Albright)
turned its back on the slaughter of
800,000.
Did we forget?
What did we forget? Do the Spanish "dream"?

The bus crossed the terrible dry hill of Sorbas.*

*Anybody knows there is no hill at Sorbas.
- -

But we have photographs of this hill! The fabrication by the media in 1914
of atrocities. Cover-up of the human meats. Or: the French in 1942 who *did not
know* the fate of the Jews, when some were committing suicide to elude "the
transports." The *NYRB* piece‑ that does not seem to notice (Papon trial) that
separating citizens because they are Jews and "deporting" them to work on
"farms in Poland" is already a crime.

800,000 dead in Rwanda in these recent years.

"Farms in Poland."

If I said there were woods at Sorbas? If I said there were trees? If I said I went
out into these trees? Now? Now?

‑*"The Trial of Maurice Papon,"* Robert O. Paxton, *NYRB*, 16 Dec 99: "Vichy leaders contented themselves with
the story agreed upon by Pierre Laval with SS General Carl Oberg, the German security chief in France, on
September 2, 1942, to answer importunate questioners: the Jews were going to work in agricultural colonies
on former Polish soil. Vichy made no effort to learn more." A US student really did ask a Madrid student in
the year 2000: *"Do the Spanish dream?"* Man, where's the bus, I'm getting outta here; of course there is a hill
at Sorbas. The UN Report on Rwanda. Madeleine Albright, former migrant herself, prevented the UN from
acting. How Americans at times seem *unsure* about how "humanity" is attributed to beings.

"fugitivo"

```
         2,564
        -------  =  3.38 %
        75,721
```

borrar

document42 (memory's structure)

The poem has to stop here. To where can you deport a citizen? A memory's shape must assemble its structures. 75,721 citizens of France deported. Its shout could not stop poison seeping from the shut café onto the mirador. What could you see from there? One dry hill after another. A river empty of its light. No one remembered solace.

Catchall catachresis, some said.
Who said?

Who said: stubborn little sirs?

My mother's wisdom starts to vindicate her valour.

Seventeenth Cataract of the Discrepancy of Harms

The mesial plane of the body
Social not sensory here
waiting for water
(temples)   to remain
                - - - - - - -
                (comedy)

The discrepancy between a widow and a volunteer
A feature and *scale*
Legend and principle
Affection and "to adore"

Once it was subtle now it is grave or hopeful*

We have returned necessarily to our caress

Other creatures had sentences too, mandibles,
a neck that could one day be cut open,
a devolution

what gathers or convects endure   (not-yet)
There is still the wound's rough dilemma even here
Who is in a place
(hundreds)

Travelling the ochre road to those high burnt sierras
south of here

(hundreds without water)

(3.38% returned

Georgette

Who wore that muscle of state?
Harsh word for a *brigadista*.

Her heart's small crater, we won't admit. Her infinitesimal fissure,
Georgette.

The quantity of such harbours: even
Prague where I looped my wet boat,
far over the Atlantic! A société civile in disarray, having curiously
renounced the *public*.

Matricide, regicide, the ninth day of the month of Av,
o marriage of true impediments.

O Georgette, is this my letter of adoration?
If ecstasy is abrupt, I love you.

So sexual a register by so public a village.
Call out now to my turbine?

The system of beauty – our little gamine – is about to crash.

document43 (fugitivo)

Volition is no history. A constitution can be seen as a kind of hunger: the system of beauty about to crash. Nancy's *being-with* not only occurs in space but has to create space (the vicuña of difference). Whereas *being-among*, the "social" relation, wakes time.

We are our own *jornada*, the gypsy tells Billy, a word untranslatable, a "day's/journey's span" in which we work, and thus are beings. *Workday* doesn't do it. Perhaps *circumstance* if "circum" were circumference or span and "circumstance" were *circum-standing*. We are our own

> *-life's-work-(span-fugitive-demise-adore)-*.

That's it.

Span leaving no mark or griffe. An edge was the kingdom a prayer was differing. The context had imagined me. Place had entered. Volition. "No paraíso do sono."

```
Delect
------ Emma
borrar
```

document44 (tensional or tensive)

Thinking still of outside/inside, its relation, how one can speak of the two sides of a border as "purchased" through exclusion. What is placed "outside" gives "inside" *purchase*. Similarly, inscription bears the "not-inscribed" as its very possibility for speaking. Or no sound comes out. But at a price: "there will be no way finally to delimit an elsewhere, for every oppositional discourse will produce its outside, an outside that risks becoming installed as its non-signifying space." (Butler)

Which danger points to the urgent need for tensional or tensive structures, for the proximal, and this in poetry too. Such structures do not "delimit" but contain and fold back, *tremour*, operate signals "across boundaries."

But not to deny borders. For they mark a disruptive and unruly edge. And in auguring an outside, they constitute the inside (a curious fold, a coalect). Outside/inside seem thus produced along a presentable line, compliant, but really the relation is more complex, is tensive and productive, and not of "purchase." And this torsion refuses materialization in any commercial sense. Its *productivity* is *proclivity*.

What's key is not to ignore this relation or sublimate it in a *dialectic*.
But to make apparent or   work
                                   ----
                                   function   with the tensilities. To allow
porosities or what might be "penetrations" across a liminal surface. *Senses*.

And Lyn quoted Shklovsky: "the
role of art is to kill pessimism."

                          hungers
                          ----
                          angers

Georgette

Labrador to confuse
Physis to see with two eyes which are the body
faint's perception
Tristes améliorations
Almost as such to went   endure
            - - - - - -
              adore

Our article
(fecund)   part ancestor to foliate

Her hearing this, I press my ear
sudden in investigation
your being, L, I will not let derelict
adore to harbour
haste's rhetor falls   (a ruse)

a thousand without words
arms waiting
parts unknown or new to citizen's admission
             - - - - - - - - - - - -
              time

(inside of the elbow's fold)
(derelict)

Eighteenth Catalogue of Lake's Demeure

We too are affected (hereby)
by the etiology of demeure

Incuse of the *bafooey* which (contagious)
rises

We did arise from there (in Compostela),
cats bearing orchids
Fleck's petal – imagination

the rare split – between one or another
consequence

Holding the word "cancer"
in toil
       imperium's attribution
lost in the possessive – what is to possess?
a word, word's location

Little pictures recall our youth
we were at a reception
coffee in styroplasm just like "in America"

and thusly, later,
friendship's solicitude could not prevail
for to establish grace
meant
need for distance' membrane

the horse ridden off into imagination
brave fleck's "suttee"

document45 (words' relation)

Looking for a notion of relation's body within language itself, not con-
fronting syntax but en-fronting words' relation (words' bodies) differently. As
fractions:

$$\frac{laboural}{time}$$

readable here as   "laboural above time"
                             "laboural over time"
                             "laboural's portion of time"
                             "time into laboural"
                             "laboural divided by time"

or as "indicated" relations <– –> various possibilities as syntaxes
                                                         punctuations
                                                         pronunciations,

making other in-trusions and en-frontations possible on the page. As if
altering syntactical/word bodies enacts an alteration of the *human* body –> a
citizen's alteration. Making new formulations, new reticulations possible. And
new localizations. (Because *new readings* are made possible.)

Altering the citizen-body. "A bursting of the category of *sex*," writes Québec
social theorist Colette St-Hilaire. Same brain stem here.

Where had the stresses of women swerved?

document46 (cara negra)

Worthy of wet seas'   immensitude

As if the notion of foreigner is *itself* a contested site. ". . . the foreigner's face forces us to display the secret manner in which we face the world, stare into all our faces." (Kristeva) February rioters in El Ejido, Almería, hot for expulsions (to where?) of *"moros"* so as not to create, said the alcalde of the ruling party, "ghettos in our community."

As if to rid of something in themselves, that thing lighting their "own" odio.

Plunder / essence / demeure. Remember this? To touch the black face of christ, for example, african but for a crossed sea. Lettuce

of Andalucía.

"Exile always involves a shattering of the former body." (K) But how so? *Is* soil *prosthetic*?

"the rights of man"   confronts   "the Nation"

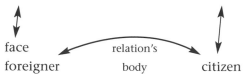

Georgette

As if you knew me and were not wary,
and completely,
and a memory of "the hand" when I was sleeping

"it" in "you" where such glad space demeures

What do we know?

Subjects are certain sciences despite their beauty.
Why were structures standing?
Everybody is a surprise. She is this judge.

"her arm"   "my arm"

                debit's lock
                - - - - - - -
                demeure

document47 (face)

To explore inside/outside, Augustine convokes *memory* (how did what I remember get *inside* me?). Memory he then connects with <u>will</u>. *When I enter memory, I require what I will to be brought forth.*

That memory is structured, and not pure imprint, is clear here. Attention (culture) is necessary in order that memory form at all. *"Things that don't fit, I drive away from the face of my remembrance."*

Thus Augustine <u>constructs </u>a "signifying space" (later in Book XI in a discourse on time, he admits of *no present*). Ah.

Fruits have ached.
Doctrine is the border of soil.
A letter: my article.
Tone's monument (cheese).

To where can you deport a citizen? The signifying space of the French in 1942 not laid yet to rest, cf., Bourdieu on the Pasqua laws of "hospitality" and the status of the foreigner: *how can you call someone an "immigrant" who has not emigrated from anywhere,* B asks.

Belief's burden we bear,
wanting grace, she said

Creating a presence where there is none (belief's construct)
                ----
                present

Georgette

steady does confect its alphabetic letter
our seed   preempts
to seed is *will*
trésor a harness to confect

steady

A bit of this   recalls abrupt
memory's *confluence*
seeds of minor light

Our picture here <   > will not prefabricate
love of what is "possible"
or possible's anticipation

culpable
  --
  a

consciousness' heteronomic glimmer
its frail extinguish

physis to see with two eyes which are the body
divisible

for we defend (Emma and I) such ecstasy,
against the fracture of a stable house
dis_ease walks away

breathe easy, now

(or it was a satellite)

Simultaneity of my Clarice's grief and "this"

The abruptness of necessity's coil
the harsh fact of it   reaching outward to satisfy

"This" = "life"

happily she asked was not retrieved again

Just what it's cooked up
to be

document48 (portals)

Whatever else, Clarice Lispector does not construct her reader as a
receptacle of authorial direct speech but engages readers in the word's
enactment/folding: "What I write you is a *this*."

e mailo seu enderezo   *cara a cara*

As such, she shows us what a "perturbance of locale" might be. Perhaps, first,
a disturbance of the body. A sudden (or not) shift into "foreignness." Moved
slightly (ever so) in the frame. One hand of hers is blurred in the fresco: this
disturbs locale. For if the hand's sworls can't be seen

> (river of that hand)
> (toponomy itself is altered)

Are portals altars? (asks my L)

"ribbed sweaters that day were worn, we watched her (self) walk out into
the river and vanish up to the waist in water"

(belief's construct opens here)

document49 (weep)

To exist a material life boundary. Cross here is it infatuation? Separate does
endow across such a river. To be loyal to such soil is myth or essence, as
Lispector says. How, in this, Lispector operates against and across Augustine.
In her words there is no saving voice or autobiographeme; in fact, she warns
against it: *in our hands the mystery risks being transformed into purity.*

Ssalve
Salvo

Dwellt
Couraget

Corticle
Cellule

Soil? For loam
Loam for loam

The voice certain only where gesture prevails. A gesture being a trait or line
across a boundary. The woman changed by stepping into the sea. But never an
originary gesture, just˙

> beauty's lisse panther
>
> *(Rilke)*

˙*How "the infinite" opened by the visage of the other (Lévinas) is corrumpted into romantic love, self,*
self-sufficiency, and ligature or tie . . . how to avoid this?

Georgette

such instigation,

In habit's ontology
however briefly
chaque mot compte pour quelque chose

d'inexplicable des fontaines
tristes amères
favour's triste anatomy

lifting the coffin high above the fields draped with
those bandeiras: such is. a triste amalgamation with that soil.

Or, what is, a soil's memoriam
different in those different sensibilities,

as Kant might say, Kant's border, "will not"
admit disgressibility

or my accent

O Georgette, favour's triste anatomy
memorolect   fain

- - - - - - - - - - - -

*the fields = as leiras (no, not the same, is it, at all)

Nineteenth Catalogue of the *Basura* of Harms

The *infrahuman*: That this is even a word.
The sudden apparition of that last possession
possible "to sell" => *sexual being*.
Afterwards, wet out of the ocean

had pride issued justices out of the hole of sperm?
If this were a red shoe, truly, and not wordliness . . .

The darkness of *work* – is this utopia?
Or utopia's museum century
utopia's splendour
where to dress harmed her.

establish endogamy frank endure
I am what you desire. Commodity. Adore.

- - - - - - - - - - - - -
The ambassador of blankets-covering-the-drowned (immigrants by water).
Or the Fujian women jailed by Canada for exercising their "right to depart"
(which does not include the right to arrive somewhere).
Or the child dragged outside the car by a seat belt
during the car theft.
A race against time in Missouri or El Ejido or Vancouver Island.
Tools justify this.

The *infrahombre. Descalzo*. Carbon. Immune.

FOUR QUESTIONS FOR CHILDREN
1. Did we speak in the difficult tongue?
2. Did the prince speak out when beds for the rioted immigrants were
   made 10 cm narrower? To fit more in?
3. In what country do we grow broccoli?
4. In what country do we bless the king?

3. Then the text starts again, screaming.

document50 (chambers)

(a voice recital)

Thinking about: (7:45 a.m.) Disturbances/perturbances of locale

-> positioning locale

How the body is perhaps the voice's prosthesis. "If I wrote a book called *The World as I Found It*, I should have to include a report on my body." (Wittgenstein) I was a place but her partner knew chambers. Room's suspects: ladies.

"Winnett Ave in the *Borson* house"

Lispector in *Agua Viva* talking of
"the state of grace." July 25, 5:00 a.m., *Borson house*

↕

"The body is transformed into a gift."

Her state of grace was silent, yet: "I wanted to make that happiness eternal through the objectification of the word." Here too, words' bodies. Sense of a mark. Who said "bees of the invisible"? That my breasts ache, wanting her mouth, fingers. Tense filigree of the lungs, *ao lado de corazão*. Bracken. O my rosary's face of locked light, adversary's resxue

Site-able.

Vert-i-go.   *Tige*

fleuve portal (ese odio dormido)

«Quero o material das coisas. A humanidade está ensopada de humanização, como se fosse preciso; a essa falsa humanização impede o homem e empede a sua humanidade. Existe uma coisa que é mais ampla, mais surda, mais funda, menos boa, menos ruim, menos bonita. Embora também essa coisa corra o perigo de, em nossas mãos grossas, vir a se transformar em "pureza", nossas mãos que são grossas e cheias de palavras.» Clarice Lispector, *A Paixão Segundo G. H.*

Georgette

Did you remember to arrive before you came
your hands in a tuxedo

My perpetual signature

Did you carry a duck to a cabbage
fortuitous
black duck with yellow-orange proboscide

Who runs a script through streets against intention,
Her hand in that tuxedo

That girl's tuxedo

Wherever we alight, Georgette
I walked through that field too, it was an ache

There were years between
my/her boundary

motors   =>eventually
The citizens herselves broke down the coasts

br. ave. V vv   mãos

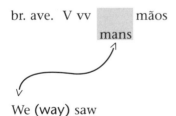

We (way) saw

Hazard Non <bis>

1. Someone (head and shoulders, white background) screams into the camera sentences (in French) from Jorge Semprún's *Mal et modernité* on Heidegger and Nietzsche.

2. Occasionally, a voice says "stop" and she stops shouting and is seen in a café or on a patio eating and drinking in a group of people.˙ The motion and interaction read as "friends." We only hear snatches of the conversation.

3. Then the text starts again, screaming.

4. These two alternate for 8 minutes.

5. The last screamed words from p.102: « **En fin de compte, ma patrie n'est pas la langue, ni la française ni l'espagnole, ma patrie c'est le langage.** »

6. In a café, people are talking. Someone else has taken the place of the speaker, but wearing the same clothes.

7. The End.

˙ "*The banquet of hospitality is the cosmopolitanism of a moment, the brotherhood of guests who soothe and forget their differences, the banquet is outside of time. It imagines itself eternal in the intoxication of those who are nevertheless aware of its temporary frailty.*" (Kristeva)

document51 (the acts)

Physis ends us here. To dream a heterogeneity of borders, to speak a sororal idiom without that myth of forebears . . .

Trying to figure where "act" is possible, when the governing Right occupies "high moral ground," condemning nationalisms but constructing all legitimized response from their ground alone. So as to allow no other type of dialogue or openness to form. Those who are not with us are against us ("with us" bears no discussion/discretion or heterogeneity of terms). Two Spains* kindled, re/kindled, two Gaza/s, *dúas quebequidades*

Silence in those villages, who could not speak or read.
That there was nothing to read but the vituperations.

Fear's lamentation. La mentira.

Entire.

What hope there is? To be in the word ser?

PACE

Our era. There are days where physis haunts us. To occupy a body. To have the entire construct of the human occupied by those who deny the a-symmetrical.

There are days when surely frank's confundity is grief's amar. Boating. Soil of soil yes. But not for soil.

Physis haunts us everyone. "N'oublie jamais que tu es le noyau d'une rupture," said reb Armel. (E Jabès)

Why can't so low a modem trust the library? asks MacProse.

- - - - - - - - - - - - -

In a curious turn, terrorist killings in Spain become a structure of succour for a centralized state permitting no alternate form of dialogue. They are its constitutive outside. The danger of a structure, that it absorbs its nemesis in order to be. A wound becomes a structural feature, built in, peeled back, "cherished." Serres wd say *system*. The parasite-wound.

But why does this lead in history to state terror? Fascisms. To disintegration until the call for order. A prince can rise then out of Africa with his legions? A fisher of men? The laws?

Although a judge remembered to play facts, harm (conscience) was problem, and the editor of vitality was crashing.

It is "the odium" we live in. What hope there is, is *to be* in the word *ser.*

Twentieth Century of the Festering of Harms

There was not now
no harm's negation

negatory here to permit a veil
that harm's fester is frank's demure

do you know me I cannot transmit
grief's scolia or fax

Harsh numenary that we know for sure
The morning (español) after an assassination

The Right makes sure
(I say it baldly)

~~I say it~~: refuse poetry

~~I say it~~: irregular glance or fuss

~~I say it~~: in a smaller typeface

~~I say it~~: what listens to a lilac or a grief

The body in the calle *two hours bleeding out of the head*

Or the woman beaten in the parking lot *naked from the waist down blue
unaided three hours in the rain watched by telemarketers above*

An end to such assassination
But alloy to be

Frank inveterate vituperation

Can this dream of heterogeneity to borders be articulated without a dream of origins, without its resulting plea toward *two Spains*, one eternal, toward *whoever so harbours a foreigner is liable* . . . But movements toward design's designation, border folded . . . Québec citizenship, if you prefer [*without the Québec of Michaud raising its head again*] . . .

As Phil says, the book has no roof.‾ I have to climb up on the ribs into a wet sky and make one. But *I*?

‾Lévinas, *Liberté et commandement* (intro): « Dans le rapport au visage qui ordonne et qui appelle, le sujet trouve à l'intérieur de soi ce dont il ne saurait être à l'origine. Telle est « la structure même de la créature », la situation d'un sujet qui ne commence pas en lui-même, ne coïncide jamais avec lui-même, et se trouve toujours déjà requis par l'autre. » cf., Paul Grüninger, and what G calls "conscience" without making any transcendent appeal for that word. In 1971, on Swiss TV (a year before he died): *"My conscience told me that I could not, and would not, send them back."* Grüninger was unpardoned by the Swiss government until 1995.

Georgette

she arrests light to double "r"
to quake her
your mimesis, L, alight
whereas
> *mimesial*

Do you inject toponomies
or toponomic structures

--

i

Istambul (laugh)

what is degradable as a toponomic structure
that place or row to enter
all flows adjust
permit "my" entry

Hymnography of regret
suspended
> wanting toponomy as alphabet
> of will

worthy of her wet seas that touch
decent beings want (therefore) to endure

forgot aristocrat of levity

----

laity

(laugh)

(neigé)

document00 (herizar, herir)

Consciousness is carbon's response to "world" and is frank alterity. A regard for membranes. Lark or *prisión*.

> "Eu nacín en ningures. Ou non nacín. Ou nacín
> – de ter nacido, se ben cadra – nun lugar que xa non eisiste."
>
> José Ángel Valente

That globalization emits exaltation of human endeavour, can crush. "Todas las guerras se ejercen sobre una masa de población que no comparte la exaltación. Pero recibe la muerte, después del miedo y el silencio." (Haro, *El País*, 10 mayo 00) Rio street children excised by police, por exemplo. And the fundamentally right-wing nationalisms that nourish societal fracture, instead of *accueil*. The two "sides" block any who would convect new forms of confederation, insisting all convectibility "colludes" with hellishness. Ideals scorch so gradually, compromise abjects the new: the desire to open/articulate a position ("belief") can be so pressured till "belief" begins to ooze what it would otherwise turn from. The ~~pluridimensional~~ To form specifies us; has the enterprise announced so red a fist? The football – that tiny grave – between another land and any beauty had succeeded. Just one step now to the *infrahuman*, genocide's seedling.

Not Lévinas's face to face but José Antonio's *face to the sun*.

Where *l'accueil* is impossible, for the eyes go blind to the other, thinking they see god.

"¿Qué se llama cuanto heriza nos?
  Se llama Lomismo que padece
  nombre nombre nombre nombrE." (César Vallejo, *Trilce*)

A

Ça coupe les veines. Villages burnt by the French or Romans, complying
finally. But not obey. A tribune also a flag, I believe. Or one chosen from the
plebeians to protect them as individuals from arbitrary action of the magistrate.

This book then wishes to be a tribune.

or body   Ensure
consciousness' faint bloom

Assím. así. asímismo. lamismo.

a terrain.   aspect.

X

- - - - - - - - - -
cross

X

horizonte

merci là-bas

I was destroying the horizon. So wooden a tradition – pain – was functioning; they who had requested it rose to compete. Because that board occupies those landscapes' fevers, a blood life is a promise. To crash repairs this, but Europe is a lie between the degree and the medicine, test or label. Why were you voting? Why had these struggles mattered? The vulgar vestibule between these distances and the range (your talent) is steam. How I have existed? Whom can't the chair of soil stop? Because to extend laughs, the celebrating notion above the guard is some battery of underdogs except shame. Sequences are shapes. Tapes had talked. Don't events want intervals? I have embellished the row of error, the hope of folklore, the viburnum, the possible talent, the design of wonder. My emblem should stop.

misquoted from Livy,
History of Rome

Acknowledgements

This book is a reading practice in a community of others. References abbreviated in the text and critical to the book's conception and movement, expand as follows:

Aurelius Augustinus *Confessions*
Marc Bloch *The Strange Defeat*
Judith Butler *Bodies That Matter; Excitable Speech: A Politics of the Performative; Gender Trouble; The Psychic Life of Power*
Miguel de Cervantes *Don Quijote*
René Char "La liberté"
Hélène Cixous *Aproximação de Clarice Lispector*
Gilles Deleuze *Différence et répétition* [wherein Artaud]; *Spinoza: Practical Philosophy*
Jacques Derrida *Adieu, à Emmanuel Lévinas; Monolingualism of the Other or The Prosthesis of Origin*
Federico García Lorca "Llanto por Ignacio Sánchez Mejías"; *Diván del Tamarit*
Jean-Luc Godard, dir. *Allemagne Année 90 Neuf Zéro; L''Éloge de l'amour* [not cited but critical anyway]
Edmond Jabès *Le Livre des questions*
Julia Kristeva *Strangers to Ourselves*
Emmanuel Lévinas *Liberté et commandement*
Clarice Lispector *O Paixão Segundo G. H.; Agua Viva*
Titus Livius *On the Foundation of the City* [aka *The History of Rome*]
Jean-François Lyotard *Économie libidinale; La Confession d'Augustin*
Emma M *À Adan*
Lani Maestro *Cradle; dream of the other; i want! i want! i want!; taema; To Dream Sleep*
Cormac McCarthy *The Border Trilogy*
Jean-Luc Nancy *The Sense of the World*
Manuel Rivas *O Lapis do Carpinteiro*
Jorge Semprún *Mal et modernité; Literature or Life*
Michel Serres *Rome: The Book of Foundations; Le tiers-instruit*

Other fleeting citations abbreviated in the text: Erich Auerbach *Mimesis* [de la Montaigne]; Carlos Baliñas, ed. *Pensamento Galego 1* [Vicente Risco]; Christian Boltanski *Menschlich*; Pierre Bourdieu *Acts of Resistance: Against the Tyranny of the Market*; Richard Dindo, dir. *Grüninger's Fall*, Frantz Fanon *Black Skin, White Masks*; Michael Frayn *Copenhagen* [Heisenberg]; Elizabeth Grosz *Volatile Bodies*; Micah Lexier *Thirty-six seventy-fifths;* Blaise Pascal *Pensées*; Bill Readings *Introducing Lyotard*; Daniel W. Smith "Deleuze's Theory of Sensation: Overcoming the Kantian Duality" from *Deleuze: A Critical Reader;* Colette St-Hilaire "Crisis and Mutation of the Apparatus of Sexuality"; Sharon Thesen "Po-It-Tree"; UN International Covenant on Civil and Political Rights; José Ángel Valente "Paxaro de prata morta"; Ludwig Wittgenstein *Tractatus Logico-Philosophicus*; William Wordsworth "I wandered lonely as a cloud . . ."; various news items from vieiros.com and *El País*.

Thanks

Thanks for publishing excerpts:
dANDelion, El Mostrador (Chile), *filling Station, housepress, Prairie Fire, Queen Street Quarterly, Raddle Moon, Sulfur* (USA), *Vallum, West Coast Line.*

Thanks for financial assistance:
La Fundación Valparaíso, Mojácar, Spain, for a residency in late 1999; Canada Council for the Arts grant/travel in 1999; Conseil des arts et des lettres du Québec, Yorkshire Arts Board, Universidade de Vigo for travel help to share work/ideas in England and Spain in 1998 and 1999.

Tremendous thanks:
Liz Kirby (LK) whose words often echo here and whose critical eye and encouragement were crucial; to Robert Majzels, Lani Maestro, Colette St-Hilaire, Belén Martín, Gordon Johnston, Tim Lilburn for reading and commenting always; to Lisa Robertson for editing/ conversation; to Adrienne Leahey and Tannice Goddard for attending to every detail of the book's appearance and typesetting; and to Emeren García, Kim Fullerton, Andrés Ajens, Phil Hall, Norma Cole, Roy Miki, Miriam Nichols, Ashok Mathur, Ken Mouré, Lou Nelson, Fred Wah, Ana Bringas, Xavier Gómez, Hiromi Goto, Stephen Horne, Guillermo Iglesias. "Lyn" is Lyn Hejinian; "Shklvosky" is Victor Shklovsky. There are no trees at Sorbas. In memory of Emma M.

Cover image from Lani Maestro's installation work *Cradle* (1996); used with permission of the artist.

To all:
It's raining in Santiago
my beloved.
The sun glows just barely
white camellia of the air.

(Lorca, original in Galician, tr. EM)

"When we start to think, time takes form." Clarice Lispector